More Puzzles to Puzzle You

Original... Maddening and... Irresistible!
Here are over 300 tantalising puzzles, brain-teasers
and riddles by one of the greatest mathematical
geniuses of the twentieth century, Shakuntala
Devi, popularly known as the 'human computer'.
The puzzles include every possible type of
mathematical recreation; time and distance
problems, age and money riddles, puzzles
involving geometry and elementary algebra, and
just plain straight thinking. Often entertaining,
but always stimulating, the puzzles included in
the book offer hours of fun and relaxation.

*"Shakuntala Devi is the internationally
renowned mathematics wizard, a recent entrant
into the Guiness Book of Records, astrologer
and teacher of 'mind-dynamics'.*
Indian Express

*"Shakuntala Devi excites the admiration of all
who have ever wanted to take a sledgehammer
to a computer. Mrs. Devi's achievement — all
honour to her for it — is that she has out-
thought one of the smuggest, most supercilious
computers in the land, a Univac 1108. She has a
mind that out-Univacs Univac... Her feat
performed at Southern Methodist University,
goes into the Guiness Book of World Records."*
The Georgia State University Signal, USA

By the same author
in
Orient Paperbacks

Puzzles to Puzzle You
The Book of Numbers
Astrology for You
Perfect Murder
Figuring: The Joy of Numbers

MORE PUZZLES

Shakuntala Devi

ORIENT PAPERBACKS
A Divison of Vision Books Pvt. Ltd.
New Delhi • Mumbai • Hyderabad

ISBN 81-222-0048-6

1st Published 1985
21st Printing 2001

More Puzzles To Puzzle You

© Shakuntala Devi

Cover design by Vision Studio

Published by
Orient Paperbacks .
(A division of Vision Books Pvt. Ltd.)
Madarsa Road, Kashmere Gate, Delhi-110 006

Printed in India at
Kay Kay Printers, Delhi-110 007

Cover Printed at
Ravindra Printing Press, Delhi-110 006

Mathematical Puzzles
and
Riddles

Anyone can be a mathematician. Most people will not agree with me, I know. But I insist that any person with average intelligence can master the science of mathematics with proper guidance and training.

Mathematics is the mother of all sciences. The world cannot move an inch without mathematics. Every businessman, accountant, engineer, mechanic, farmer, scientist, shopkeeper, even street hawker requires a knowledge of mathematics in the day to day life.

Besides man, animals and insects also use mathematics in their day to day existence. Snails make shells with curious mathematical precision. Spiders produce intricacies of engineering. Honey bees construct combs of greatest strength consistent with the least possible amount of wax. There are countless mathematical patterns in nature's fabric.

God or nature, whichever one believes in, is the greatest mathematician of all. Fruits of teasle and sunflower and the scales of cones are not arranged haphazardly. A close examination would convince us that in corn and elm each leaf is halfway around the stem from the leaves immediately above and below it. If one should trace the point of attachment upwards with the aid of thread freshly coated with mucilage, it would be found that they lie on a spiral.

In plants like beech and sedge, each leaf is attached one-third of the way around the stem from leaves immediately above or below it. Another kind of spiral is found in twigs of the oak, the apple and many other plants. The leaves are two-fifths of the circumference apart and the curve, make two revolutions and goes through five attachments in passing from any leaf to the one directly over it. This would be the fraction 2/5.

Mathematical training is essential to children if they are to flourish effectively in the newly forming technological world of tomorrow. No longer it is enough to train children to meet known challenges; they must be prepared to face the unknown — because it seems certain that tomorrow won't be much like today. It is now time for us to rethink our approach to maths learning.

Experience shows that the basic principles of learning mathematics can be made easier and more fun for the clever and ordinary alike through mathematical activities and games. If mathematics can be turned into a game, it can literally become child's play. Class experience indicate clearly that mathematical puzzles and riddles encourage an alert, open minded attitude in youngsters and help them develop their clear thinking.

In the light of this aspect I have presented the puzzles, riddles and games in this book. Each puzzle, riddle or game is designed to develop some aspect of a person's inborn potential to think creatively.

I have tried to cover a wide range of mathematical topics and levels of difficulty, with an aim to pull together many different topics in mathematics. The varied kinds of levels of problems provide both a review of previous work and an introduction to a new topic as well as motivation to learn new techniques needed to solve more specialized types of problems.

The writing of this book has been a thrilling experience for me and I hope my readers will share with me this experience.

Shakuntala Devi

Puzzles Riddles & Brain Teasers

A Problem of Shopping

Meena went out for shopping. She had in her handbag approximately Rs. 15/- in one rupee notes and 20 p. coins. When she returned she had as many one rupee notes as she originally had and as many 20 p. coins as she originally had one rupee notes. She actually came back with about one-third of what she had started out with.

How much did she spend and exactly how much did she have with her when she started out?

A Question of Distance

It was a beautiful sunny morning. The air was fresh and a mild wind was blowing against my wind screen. I was driving from Bangalore to Brindavan Gardens. It took me 1 hour and 30 minutes to complete the journey.

After lunch I returned to Bangalore. I drove for 90 minutes. How do you explain it?

Smallest Integer

Can you name the smallest integer that can be written with two digits?

4

A Puzzle Of Cultural Groups

My club has five cultural groups. They are literary, dramatic, musical, dancing and painting groups. The literary group meets every other day, the dramatic every third day, the musical every fourth day, the dancing every fifth day and the painting every sixth day. The five groups met, for the first time on the New Year's day of 1975 and starting from that day they met regularly according to schedule.

Now, can you tell how many times did all the five meet on one and the same day in the first quarter? Of course the New Year's day is excluded.

One more question—were there any days when none of the groups met in the first quarter and if so how many were there?

5

The Biggest Number

Can you name the biggest number that can be written with four 1s?

6

A Problem of Regions

There are thirty-four lines that are tangent to a circle, and these lines create regions in the plane. Can you tell how many of these regions are not enclosed?

7

A Problem of Age

Recently I attended a cocktail party. There was a beautiful young woman, who also seemed very witty and intelligent. One of the other guests suddenly popped a question at her "How old are you?" For a moment she looked a bit embarrassed and while I stood there wondering how she was going to wriggle out of the situation, she flashed a charming smile and answered, "My age three years hence multiplied by 3 and from that subtracted three times my age three years ago will give you my exact age".

The man who had asked her the age just walked away puzzled. Then she leaned over and whispered to me "if he can calculate that one, he deserves to know my age."

How old do you think she was?

8

Solve a Dilemma

What is wrong with this proof?

$$2 = 1$$
$$a = b$$
$$a^2 = ab$$
$$a^2 - b^2 = ab - b^2$$
$$(a + b)(a - b) = b(a - b)$$
$$a + b = b$$
$$2b = b$$
$$2 = 1$$

9

Pursue the Problem

Simplify $(-\frac{1}{8}) - \frac{2}{3}$

as far as you can

10

A Problem of Walking

Next door to me lives a man with his son. They both work in the same factory. I watch them going to work through my window. The father leaves for work ten minutes earlier than his son. One day I asked him about it and he told me he takes 30 minutes to walk to his factory, whereas his son is able to cover the distance in only 20 minutes.

I wondered, if the father were to leave the house 5 minutes earlier than his son, how soon the son would catch up with the father.

How can you find the answer?

11

Peculiar Number

Here is a multiplication:

$$159 \times 49 = 7632$$

Can you see something peculiar in this multiplication? Yes, all the nine digits are different. How many other similar numbers can you think of?

12

A Problem of Handshakes

Recently I attended a small get-together. I counted the number of handshakes that were exchanged. There were 28 altogether.

Can you tell me how many guests were present?

13

A Problem of Cog-wheels

Here is a cog-wheel that has eight teeth. It is coupled with a cog-wheel of 24 teeth.

Can you tell how many times the small cog-wheel must rotate on its axis to circle around the big one?

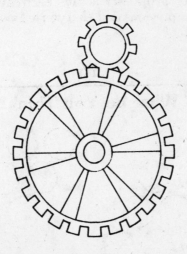

14

A Surprise!

Write 1/81 as a repeating decimal.
You're in for a surprise!

15

Some Glutton!

I was lunching in a South Indian restaurant. The place was crowded. A man excused himself and sat at my table. He began to eat idlis one after the other. As soon as one plate was finished he ordered more. As I sat there discreetly watching him, somewhat stunned, after he finished the last idli he told the waiter that he did not want any more. He took a big gulp of water, looked at me, smiled and said 'The last one I ate was the 100th idli in the last five days. Each day I ate 6 more than on the previous day. Can you tell me how many I ate yesterday?'

16

What do You Think?

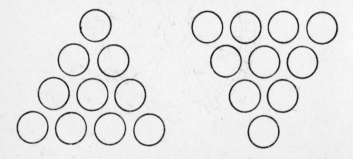

Make the left arrangement look like the right arrangement by moving only three circles from the left arrangement.

17

Sum of the Reciprocals

The sum of two numbers is ten. Their product is twenty. Can you find the sum of the reciprocals of the two numbers?

18

Bingo!

A group of us were playing Bingo. I noticed something very interesting. There were different Bingo cards with no two cards having the same set of numbers in corresponding column or row. The centre of course was a free space.

How many such cards are possible, can you tell?

19

A Combination Problem

Can you combine eight 8s with any other mathematical symbols except numbers so that they represent exactly one thousand?

You may use the plus, minus terms, and division signs as well as the factorial function and the Gamma function. You may also use the logarithms and the combinatorial symbol.

Count the Triangles

Take a good look at this sketch:

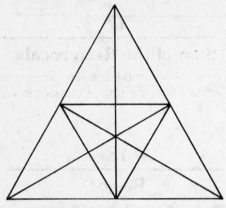

Now can you tell how many triangles are there in this figure?

No Change!

I got out of the taxi and I was paying the fare. But the taxi driver could not give me change for the rupee note. To my surprise I noticed my two friends Asha and Neesha walking towards me. I requested them to give me exact change for my rupee note. They searched their handbags and said 'No'.

They both had exactly Re 1.19 each in their handbags. But the denominations were such that they could not give the exact change for a rupee.

What denominations of change could they have had? They both, of course, had different denominations.

Find out the Sum

What is the sum of all numbers between 100 and 1000 which are divisible by 14?

23

Count the Squares

Take a good look at this figure:

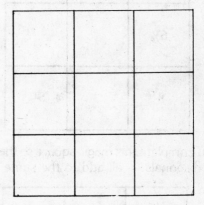

How many squares are there in this figure?

24

Something for the Chickens

A friend of mine runs a small poultry farm in Bangalore. She took me round to see the place. I counted the number of chickens. There were 27 of them. And there were 4 enclosures. I noticed that in each enclosure there were an odd number of chickens.

Can you tell how many there were in each enclosure?

25

Magic Square

13	4¼	
6¾		
8		5½

Can you complete this magic square so that the rows, columns, diagonals — all add to the same number.

	21	

18

26

Find out the Value

What is the value of
$\sqrt{12} + \sqrt{12} + \sqrt{12} + \sqrt{12} + \sqrt{12} +$

27

A Hair Raising Problem

Prof Guittierz is a very interesting person. I met him in Montevideo, Uruguay some time back. We were discussing people's hair.

Prof Guittierz told me that there are about 150,000 hairs on an average on a man's head. I disagreed with him. I told him that no one could have actually come by this figure — who would have the patience to actually take a man's head and take the hair by hair and count them!

'No' he argued 'It is enough to count them on one square centimetre of a man's head and knowing this and the size of the hair covered surface, one can easily calculate the total number of hairs on a man's head'.

Then he popped a question at me. 'It has also been calculated that a man sheds about 3000 hairs a month. Can you tell me the average longevity of each hair on a man's head?

Can you guess what my answer was?

28

Value of 'S'

If S = (1/N + 1)N
And N = 10
Compute S

Test this Square

Is this a magic square? If so why?

1	12	10
15	2	4
8	5	3

A Question of Age

Last winter I was in the United Kingdom. Travelling by train from London to Manchester, I had for company two middle-aged Englishmen who were seated opposite to me. Naturally, they did not speak to me — because we hadn't been introduced. But I could not help overhearing their conversation.

'How old is Tracy, I wonder?' one asked the other.

'Tracy!' the other replied 'Let me see — eighteen years ago he was three times as old as his son.'

'But now, it appears, he is only twice as old as his son' said the former.

I tried to guess Tracy's age, and his son's age. What do you think my solution was?

31

A Pair of Palindromes

Multiply 21978 by 4
Now see if you can find a pair of palindromes.

32

A Computing Problem

Compute :
$[5 - 2 (4 - 5)^{-1}]^2$

33

A Problem of Sari, Shoes and Handbag

When I walked into that shop in New Market I had altogether Rs 140/- in purse. When I walked out I didn't have a single paise, instead I had a sari, a pair of shoes and a handbag.

The sari cost Rs 90/- more than the handbag and the sari and the handbag cost together Rs 120/- more than the pair of shoes.

How much did I pay for each item?

34

Rule of Three

What is meant by the rule of three?

35

Compute 'M'

$8^m = 32$

36

A Matter of Denomination

One morning I went to draw some money from my bank. The Cashier behind the counter smiled at me and said 'I've got here money of all denominations. I've got denominations of 1 Paise, 5 Paise, 10 Paise, 25 Paise, 50 Paise, Re 1/-, Rs 2/-, Rs 5/-, Rs 10/-, Rs 20/-, Rs 50/-, Rs 100/-, Rs 500/- and Rs 1000/-.

How many different amounts of money can I make by taking one or more of each denomination?

What do you think my answer was?

37

Count the Digits

Can you find a number which added to itself one or several times will give a total having the same digits as that number but differently arranged and after the sixth addition will give a total of all nines?

38

Prime Number

Do you know which is the largest known prime number?

39

A Computing Problem

Compute x if: $X = \dfrac{1}{1.2} + \dfrac{1}{2.3} + \dfrac{1}{3.4} + \dfrac{1}{4.5} + \dfrac{1}{5.6} + \dfrac{1}{6.7}$

$+ ... \dfrac{1}{(n-1)n} + \dfrac{1}{n(n+1)}$

40

Wrong Names of Months

It was in Vienna that I met Prof. Jellinek. He was a linguist. We were discussing calendars for some time — Gregorian calendar, Julian calendar, Hindu calendar, Chinese calendar etc. Then suddenly he popped this question at me.

'Don't you think it is strange. December is the twelfth month of the year. And do you know what actually December means — ten! 'Daka' is a Greek word meaning ten. Therefore, decalitre would mean ten litres and decade means ten years. December then should be the tenth month. But it isn't. How do you explain it?

What do you think my answer was?

41

A Rotating Wheel

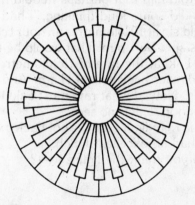

Here is a wheel with a fixed centre. Assuming that the outside diameter is of six feet, can you tell how many revolutions will be required so that a point on its rim will travel one mile?

42

Continue the Series

1, 3, 6, 10
Name the next three numbers in the series

43

A Problem of Skiing

It was a skiing resort in Switzerland. I met a skiing enthusiast by the skiing slopes. He had a packed lunch with him. He asked me to join him for lunch back in the spot where we were standing at 1 p.m., after he had done a bit of skiing. I told him no, as I had an appointment to keep at 1 p.m. But if we could meet at 12 noon, I told him that perhaps I could manage.

Then he did some loud thinking, "I had calculated that if I could ski at 10 kilometres an hour I could arrive back at this spot by 1 p.m. That would be too late for you. But if I ski at the rate of 15 kilometres an hour, then I would reach back here at 11 a.m. And that would be too early. Now at what rate must I ski to get back here at 12 noon?....let me see".

He got the right figure and he got back exactly at 12 noon. We had an excellent lunch.

What do you think the figure was?

44

Smallest Positive Prime

Which is the smallest positive prime which is some multiple of seven less than a cube of a counting number less than ten?

45

Sum of the Coefficients

Find the sum of the coefficients if:
$(a + b)^{29}$ is expanded.

46

A Puzzle of Numbers

It was a rainy Sunday afternoon. I took shelter inside a friend's house. He was entertaining a group of people. I joined the group. We were discussing numbers and their interesting qualities. Then my friend who is a mathematician said that he would show us something very interesting.

He gave me a piece of paper and asked me to write any three digit number.

'Can there be any zeros in it?' I asked.

'Any number, using any digit from zero to nine. But don't show me the number' he said.

I wrote down a three digit number and asked him what to do next.

'Fold the paper and pass it on to the man next to you' he said.

'What do I do?' Asked the man next to me.

'Write the same number along side and pass it on to your neighbour' he said.

25

'Now you've got a six digit number. Divide this number by seven' he said to the man who had the paper.

'What if it doesn't divide? What if it leaves a fraction?' asked that man.

'It will, don't worry' said my friend.

'But how do you know? You haven't even seen the number'.

'Leave that to me. Just divide, tear a piece of paper, write the result on it and pass it on to the man next to you.'

When the next man got the number, my friend asked him to divide the number by 11 and pass on, only the result to the next man. The next man was now asked to divide the number by 13.

'This time, I am sure the number will not divide by 13. Very few numbers do' he said.

'That's my headache. You just go ahead and do the division' said my friend.

'Good god. It does divide by 13. I was just lucky' remarked the man with the slip.

'Now write down the result in another bit of paper. Fold it many times over so that I do not see the number and give it to me' said my friend.

When he got the folded bit of paper, he handed it over to me and asked, 'Is this the number you wrote down to start with?'

I was amazed! It was exactly the three digit number I had written at the outset.

How do you explain it?

47

Don't Cross the Lines

Here is a sketch with three squares.

Can you draw a line in these three squares in one continuous line without crossing any lines or taking the pencil off the paper?

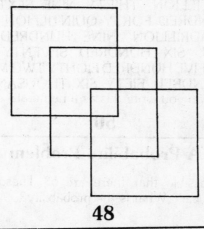

48

Do You have Change?

Can you change a rupee note in such a way that there are exactly fifty coins? No 2 Paise coins.

49

Abra Cadabra

SEVEN VIGINTILLION, THREE HUNDRED FORTY SIX NOVEMDECILLION, SIX HUNDRED FORTY EIGHT OCTODECILLION, FOUR SEPTEDECILLION, FIVE HUNDRED SIXTY SEXDECILLION, NINE HUNDRED EIGHTYSIX

QUINDECILLION, TWO HUNDRED FIFTEEN QUATTOUR DECILLION, THREE HUNDRED FORTY EIGHT DUODECILLION, FOUR HUNDRED FORTY FOUR UNDECILLION, TWO HUNDRED EIGHTYSIX DECILLION, FOUR HUNDRED FORTY FIVE NONILLION, THREE HUNDRED AND FIVE OCTILLION, ONE HUNDRED FORTY SIX SEPTILLION, THIRTY NINE SEXTILLION, ONE HUNDRED FORTY QUINTILLION, FORTY SIX QUADRILLION, NINE HUNDRED SIXTY TRILLION, SIX HUNDRED SEVENTY EIGHT BILLION, FIVE HUNDRED EIGHTY TWO MILLION, TWO HUNDRED FIFTY SIX THOUSAND AND THREE. Can you write this as a numeral?

50

A Probability Problem

Is it possible that there are 53 Tuesdays in a non-leap year? What is the probability?

51

Volume of a Cylinder

A cylindrical container has a radius of eight inches with a height of three inches. Compute how many inches should be added to either the radius or height to give the same increase in volume?

52

Little Mammu and the String

'Mummy give me more string, I want to play telephone with Naval' said my little girl Mammu.

'More string, good god! I gave you so much this morning. What did you do with the whole ball I gave you?' I exclaimed.

'Oh you took back half of what you gave me to its packages' Mammu countered.

'You still have the other half of the ball'.

'Deepa took half of what remained, to pack some books and toys'.

'And what about the rest?'

'There was very little left and Amit took half of what I had to fix his suspenders. Then Pallavi took two-fifths of what was remaining to tie her pony tail'.

'I see'.

'Now all I have left is 30 centimetres. Can I possibly play telephone with 30 centimetres?'

How much string did I give Mammu in the first place?

53

Tail or Head

Supposing six coins are flipped, what is the probability of at least getting one tail?

54

A Division Problem

Can you divide 1000 into two parts such that one part is a multiple of 47 and the other a multiple of 19?

Count the Squares

Guess how many squares are there in this figure.

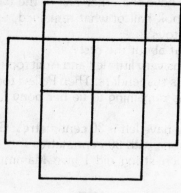

The Case of the Missing Digit

A friend of mine asked me to write down any multidigit number. But, he put a condition, the number should not end with a zero.

I put down the number 96452

Then he asked me to add up the five digits and subtract the total from the original number.

I did and here is what I got:

96452 - 26 = 96426

He then asked me to cross out any one of the five digits and tell him the remaining numbers. I crossed out the 2 and told him the rest of the digits. I neither told him the original number nor what I had done with it. Yet 'pop' he told me the exact number I had crossed out.

How do you explain it?

Magic Star

Take a good look at this six-pointed figure. This is what is known as a magic star. The total in every row adds up to the same.

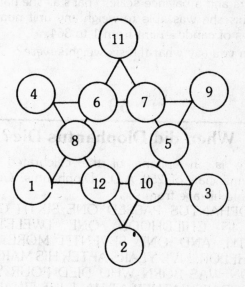

$1 + 12 + 10 + 3 = 26$ $9 + 5 + 10 + 2 = 26$
$4 + 6 + 7 + 9 = 26$ $11 + 6 + 8 + 1 = 26$
$4 + 8 + 12 + 2 = 26$ $11 + 7 + 5 + 3 = 26$

But there is something imperfect about this star. The sum of the numbers at the points do not add upto 26. Now can you replace the numbers in such a way that their sums in every row and every point add upto 26?

58

A Problem of Weights

It was Mammu's birthday and I decided to buy for her some sweets. There was an old woman in the candy shop. I noticed something very strange, while she was weighing out the sweets. She had just six wieghts and a balance scale. That's all she had. With just this she was able to weigh any unit number of ounces of candy—right from 1 to 364.

Can you say what the six weights were?

59

When did Diophantus Die?

Here is an epitaph of the celebrated Greek mathematician of 250 A.D., Diophantus. Can you calculate his age from this?

DIOPHANTUS PASSED ONE SIXTH OF HIS LIFE IN CHILDHOOD, ONE TWELFTH IN YOUTH, AND ONE SEVENTH MORE AS A BACHELOR; FIVE YEARS AFTER HIS MARRIAGE A SON WAS BORN WHO DIED FOUR YEARS BEFORE HIS FATHER AT HALF HIS FINAL AGE. HOW OLD IS DIOPHANTUS?

60

Pin-Point the Time

At this moment it is 9 P.M. Can you tell me what time it will be 23999 999 992 hours later?

61

Question of Probability

My friend Parveen teaches at a school. One day she conducted a test for three of her students and when they handed back the test papers, they had forgotten to write their names.

Parveen returned the papers to the students at random.

What is the probability that none of the three students will get the right paper?

62

How Big Will it Look?

We have an angle of $1\frac{1}{2}°$ How big will it look through a glass that magnifies things three times?

63

A Problem of Gifts

It was Diwali day. A day to exchange gifts. Two fathers gave their sons some money. One father gave his son Rs. 150/- and the other Rs. 100/-. But when the two sons counted their money, they found that between them they had become richer by only Rs. 150/-.

How do you explain this?

64

Find out the Value

Can you figure out?

33

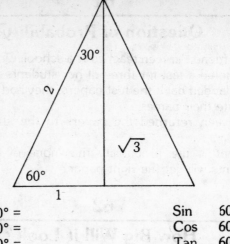

Sin 30° =   Sin 60° =
Cos 30° =   Cos 60° =
Tan 30° =   Tan 60° =
Ctn 30° =   Ctn 60° =
Sec 30° =   Sec 60° =
Csc 30° =   Csc 60° =

65

Height of a Pole

What will be the height of a pole made up of all the millimetre cubes in one cubic metre, if placed one on top of another?

66

Volley of Questions

Here are a set of questions. Try to figure out the answers:

a) Is there a largest pair of twin primes?

b) Is there always at least one prime between two successive perfect squares?

c) Is there a largest even perfect number?

d) Is there a formula in terms of N, where N is any natural number, that will only generate primes for all N?

e) Is Fermat's last theorem true or false? His last theorem states that 'The equation $x^n + y^n = 2^n$ where 'n' is an integer greater than two, has no solution in positive integers.

f) Is it possible that somewhere in the decimal approximation for pi there occur seven consecutive seven e.g. = 3.14159 ...7777777

g) Is it possible that every even number greater than two can be written as the sum of exactly two primes?

h) Is it possible that if the ratio of the number of twin primes less than N to the number of primes less than N approaches some limit as N gets larger and larger?

i) Is it possible that the series of Mersenne primes continues for ever, or has a largest member?

j) What is the best way to pack the most spheres into a given container with a given volume?

k) Is it possible that there exists maps that require five different colours so that two countries with a common boundary have different colours?

l) Is it possible that there are odd perfect numbers?

m) Is it possible that there exist a pair of available numbers of opposite parity—one odd, one even.

67

Cutting the Face of a Clock

Here is the face of a clock.

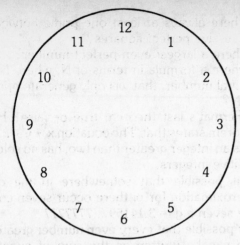

Can you cut the face of the clock into six parts of any shape in such a way that the aggregate number in all of them is the same?

This problem is a sure test of your ingenuity and resourcefulness.

68

Beetles and Spiders

Naval collected 8 spiders and beetles into a little box. When he counted the legs he found that there were altogether 54.

How many beetles and how many spiders did he collect?

69

Value of 'S'

S434S0 What number must be substituted with 'S' to make it divisible by 36?

70

Read out the Figure

A London monument is marked as follows:

MDCLXVI

What year does it represent?

71

Rupees One Hundred For Rupees Five

Recently I attended a magic function. The magician made a very attractive proposal from the stage:

'Can anyone in the audience give me Rs 5/- in 20 coins. One condition. The coins must be of 50P, 20P and 5P denominations. No other coins would do. To anyone who can give me this I am willing to give away Rs 100/-. One hundred rupee for five!'

Every one was silent. No one went forward. Some people began to look for bits of papers and pencil in their pockets evidently to calculate their chances. But no one went forward.

The magician renewed his offer once again. 'What, no takers. No one wants to make easy money!'

There was silence in the auditorium.

'Perhaps you think it is too much to give me Rs 5/- in exchange of Rs 100/-. Alright I'll take only Rs 3/-. Of course, in the same denominations as I mentioned already. Twenty coins. How about that now?'

No one stirred.

'Alright, alright! The magician went on. 'Even three rupees you think is too much to exchange for Rs 100/-. I will come down even more. Only two rupees—just two rupees' he showed his two fingers 'for rupees one hundred'. You can't let go of such an opportunity, really. Ladies and gentlemen. Just two rupees—in the denomination I mentioned already—twenty coins—for rupees one hundred!'

Nothing happened. He renewed his offer several times and finally he gave up.

Why do you think no one came forward to take advantage of the magician's most attractive proposal?

72

A Curve called Helen!

Can you tell what curve has been called the 'Helen of Geometers'?

73

A Prime Number Game

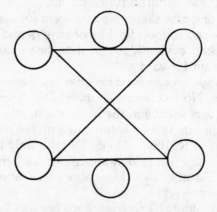

Here are seven prime numbers: 5,7,11,13,17,19,23

Can you arrange these prime numbers in the seven circles so that the rows and diagonals add upto the same prime number?

74

Three Digit Number

$153 = 1^3 + 5^3 + 3^3$

Can you find some other three digit numbers like this?

75

Interesting Sums

What is interesting about the following sum:

a) $1 + 3 + 5 = ?$
b) $1 + 3 + 5 + 7 = ?$
c) $1 + 3 + 5 + 7 + 9 = ?$
d) $1 + 3 + 5 + 7 + 9 + 11 = ?$
e) $1 + 3 + 5 + 7 + 9 + 11 + 13 = ?$
f) $1 + 3 + 5 + 7 + 9 + 11 + 13 + 15 = ?$
g) $1 + 3 + 5 + 7 + 9 + 11 + 13 + 15 + 17 = ?$
h) $1 + 3 + 5 + 7 + ...289 + 291 + 293 + 295 = ?$
i) $1 + 3 + 5 + 7 + 9 + 11 + 13...... + R = ?$

76

Pentagon in a Circle

How can you inscribe a pentagon in a given circle?

77

A Problem of Typing

It was a day of rush. I had to send off the typescript to my publisher by the evening's mail. Mr Das Gupta, my stenographer is a very experienced person and he,

I knew could do the job neatly and quickly. But even he would take 2 hours to finish the job. This couldn't have done! So I decided to engage another typist. She would do a neat job, I was told, but she was not a fast typist like Mr Das Gupta. She looked at the job and said that if she were to do the entire job by herself, it would take her three hours.

I decided to let them do the job side by side.

Within how much time, can you tell, the two of them finished the work?

78

A Diwali Gathering

It was the Diwali day. And on this day we decided that my whole family should meet. The gathering consisted of one grand-father, one grand-mother, two fathers, two mothers, four children, three grand-children, one brother, two sisters, two sons, two daughters, one father-in-law, one mother-in-law, and one daughter-in-law. We were altogether seven.

How do you explain it?

79

The Property of Numbers

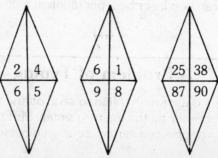

40

Take a good look at the figures in the sketches:

Each of the sets of numbers has a property concerning cubes of its elements! Can you find the property?

80

Find out the Number

Can you find a number of nine non-respective digits that is divisible by 11?

Find the smallest of such number as well as the biggest.

81

Divide the Crescent

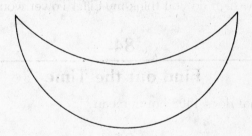

Here is a crescent.

Can you divide it into six parts by drawing just two straight lines?

82

Convert into Roman Figures

Can you write 1789 in Roman figures?

Mammu and the Eiffel Tower

Last time we were in Paris. Mammu and I—Mammu fell in love with the Eiffel Tower. She began to insist that we carry the Eiffel Tower back to India. I tried to explain to her that such a thing was impossible. But nothing would make her see reason. Finally I had to promise her that I would have an identical tower made in miniature, for her.

In order to have a smaller replica made I enquired the exact data of the Eiffel Tower Here are the details :

The Eiffel Tower is 300 metres high.

It is made of steel.

The weight of steel used is 8,000,000 kilogrammes.

I have decided to order the model to be made with only 1 kilogramme of steel.

How high do you think my Eiffel Tower would be?

84

Find out the Time

What does 1408 hours mean?

85

A Problem of Thickness

We have a large, very thin sheet of rice paper which pile at the rate of one thousand sheets to the inch Supposing we tear the paper in half and put the two pieces together, on top of each other, and we tear them in half and put the four pieces together in a pile and then we tear them again in half and put the eight pieces together in a pile, and we continue like this upto fifty times, can you tell how high the final stack of paper would be?

86

Name the Series

What is the name given to the series?

$$1 + \frac{1}{2} + \frac{1}{3} + \frac{1}{4} + \frac{1}{5} + \frac{1}{6} + \frac{1}{7} + \frac{1}{8} + \frac{1}{9}$$

87

Sum of the Angles

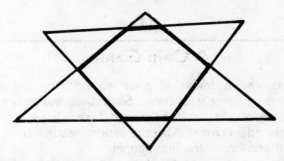

The heavy figure is a Convex Hexagon.
Can you find the sum measures of the angles A, B, C, D, E, F,.

88

Name the Series

What is the name given to the series?
0, 1, 1, 2, 3, 5, 8, 13, 21, 34, 55.....?

89

Find out the Pattern

What do you think the following pattern is?
6, 24, 60, 120, 210, 336......

90

Weight of a Brick

We have a brick of regular size. It weighs 4 kilogrammes. How much do you think a similar brick, four times smaller, but made of the same material weigh?

91

A Coin Game

Recently, a friend of mine showed me a very interesting game with coins. She asked me to bring three saucers first and she placed them in a line. Then she placed 5 coins of different denominations, one on top of another in the first saucer.

The coins were of the denominations Re 1/-, 50P, 10P, 5P and 25P and she placed the coins in the order of their size—smallest on top and biggest in the bottom.

She now asked me to transpose these coins to the third saucer observing the conditions that I transpose only one coin at a time, I do not place a bigger on a small one and I use the middle saucer only temporarily observing the first two conditions but that in the end the coins must be in third saucer and in the original order.

'Oh that's very simple. This hardly needs much effort' I said.

I took the 25P coin and put it in the third saucer. Then I kept the 5P coin in the middle saucer. Now I got stuck. I did not know where to put the 10P coin. It was bigger than both!

My friend smiled and said 'put the 25P coin on top of the 5P coin. Then you can put the 10P coin in the third saucer'.

I saw my way and did exactly what she told me. But to my great surprise I saw that my trouble had just begun. Where do I put the 50P coin?

I did a lot of thinking. I put the 25P coin into the first saucer, the 5P coin into the third and then transposed the 25P coin there two. And now I could place the 50P coin in the second saucer.

After numerous transpositions—at last—I was able to succeed in moving the entire pile of coins from the first saucer to the third.

How many moves did I make altogether?

92

Dropping a Ball

A little ball is dropped from a height of 8 ft. and it bounces back each time to a height which is one-half of the height of the last bounce

How far approximately will the ball have travelled when it comes to rest?

93

Find out the Sequence

What are the next terms in the sequence?
17, 15, 26, 22, 35, 29.......

45

Puzzle of the Matches

A friend of mine emptied a box of matches on the table and divided them into three heaps, while we stood around him wondering what he was going to do next.

He looked up and said 'well friends, we have here three uneven heaps. Of course you know that a match box contains altogether 48 matches. This I don't have to tell you. And I am not going to tell you how many there are in each heap'.

'What do you want us to do?' one of the men shouted.

'Look well, and think. If I take off as many matches from the first heap as there are in the second and add them to the second, and then take as many from the second as there are in the third and add them to the third, and lastly if I take as many from the third as there are in the first and add them to the first—then the heaps will all have equal number of matches.'

As we all stood there puzzled he asked, 'Can you tell me how many were there originally in each heap?'

Can you?

Make a Magic Square

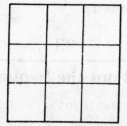

Fill in the empty squares with prime numbers and make this into a magic square.

31 1 42

96

Multiplication Problem

Naval has worked out this multiplication problem. Has he done it correctly. What is his method? Do you think this method will work in other problems in multiplication also?

$$
\begin{array}{r}
57 \\
84 \\
\hline
588 \\
420 \\
\hline
4788 \\
\end{array}
$$

97

Magic Circles

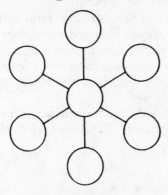

Can you place the numbers 11, 12, 13, 14, 15, 16 and 17—each number in one circle so that any three circles in a line has numbers which total the same sum?

Name Five Terms of Another Series

These are the numbers that are the first five terms of a series that add upto 150. Can you name five terms of another series without fractions that add upto 153?

10, 20, 30, 40, 50

Knitting Needle

Is a 'size 16' knitting needle twice as thick as a 'size 8' knitting needle?

A Problem of Chain Letters

I opened my mail box this morning. What do I see in it? A chain letter. This seems to turn up every now and then in one form or another.

I began to wonder. If one person sends a certain letter to two friends, asking each of them to copy the letter and send it to two of their friends, those in turn each send two letters to two of their friends and so on how many letters would have been sent by the time the letter did thirty sets.

I calculated and I had a surprise waiting for me. The answer was gigantic. What do you think the answer was?

101

Substitute the Question Marks

0, 1, 2, 3, 4, 5, 6, 7, 8, 9

$$\begin{array}{r} ?\ ?\ ? \\ +\ ?\ ?\ ? \\ \hline =\ ?\ ?\ ? \end{array}$$

Using each of the digits given above, and using each digit exactly once fill in the question marks.

102

A Problem of Ping Pong

There are 150 members in my club. We decided to have a ping pong tournament. All the members came forward to play in the game. Every time a member loses a game he is out of the tournament.

There are no ties.

Can you tell how many games must be played in order to determine the champion?

103

Missing Terms

48, 60, 58, 72, 68, 104.......
Here is a sequence. Can you find the two missing terms?

104

Measure out the Time

We have an old grandpa clock at home. It takes seven seconds for this clock to strike seven gongs. Now how long do you think it will take for striking ten gongs.

105

Packets of Candy

If 6 men can pack 6 packets of candy in 6 minutes how many men are required to pack 60 packets in 60 minutes?

106

Classify the Numbers

Here are a set of numbers:

$$161 \quad 163 \quad 167 \quad 169 \quad 187$$
$$289 \quad 293 \quad 365 \quad 367 \quad 371$$

Can you classify these numbers as prime numbers and composite numbers. And when you find a composite number, can you give its prime factors?

107

A Problem of Weight

In my neighbourhood lives a man who weighs 200 pounds. He has two sons. They both weigh 100 pounds each. On a festival day they decide to go across the river on a boat to visit some relations. But the boat could carry a maximum load of only 200 pounds.

Yet they managed to get across the river by boat. How did they?

108

Biggest Number

What is the biggest number that can be expressed in three figures?

109

Find Out

1757051

Take a good look at this number. Now tell me, is it a prime number? If not, what are its factors?

110

Mnemonic

'May I have a large container of coffee?'
This is a mnemonic. Can you tell what it signifies?

111

A Problem of Ribbon

We have a 100 ft piece of ribbon.

If it takes one second to cut it into a 1 foot strip how long would it take to cut the entire ribbon into one foot strips?

A Problem of Gooseberries

When I was a little girl, one day my mother had left a bowl of gooseberries to be shared between my two sisters Lalitha, Vasantha and myself. I went home first. I ate what I thought was my share of gooseberries and left. Then Lalitha arrived. She thought she was the first one to arrive and ate the number of gooseberries, she thought was her share and left. Lastly Vasantha arrived. She again thought she was the first one to arrive and she took what she thought was her share and left 8 gooseberries in the bowl.

When we three sisters met in the evening we realized what had happened and my mother distributed the remaining 8 gooseberries in a fair share. How did my mother do it?

113

Value of a Googol

How much is a googol?

114

Angle of Hands

The time is 2.15 P.M. What is the angle between the hour and minute hands?

115

A Problem of Candy Bars

Recently I attended a birthday party. All the children in the party were given candy bars. All the children got three candy bars each except the child sitting in the end. She got only two candy bars. If only each child had been given two candy bars there would have been eight candy bars remaining. How many candy bars were there altogether to begin with?

116

Speeding Train

The distance between Bangalore to Mysore is about 60 miles. Two trains leave at 10 in the morning. One train leaves Bangalore at 40 mph and the other from Mysore at 50 mph. When they meet are they nearer to Bangalore or Mysore?

117

Why Front Wheels Wear Out?

Perhaps you have noticed the wheels of some carts—the front ones are smaller than the rear ones. Why do the front axles wear out faster than the rear?

118

Match Sticks

Here are twelve match sticks. Can you remove exactly two so that exactly two squares remain?

119

Mathematical Oddity

In the 20th Century there are only seven years whose numbers are a mathematical oddity because their numbers signify a prime number. The first one of its kind was the year 1951. Can you name the other six?

120

Two Pumpkins

I was shopping for vegetables at the New Market. I saw two pumpkins of the same quality but of different sizes. One was bigger than the other. The bigger one was 60 cm in circumference and the other 50 cm. I asked the vendor the price. The bigger one was one and a half times more expensive. Which one do you think would have been a better buy.

121

Division of 45

Can you divide the number 45 into four parts such that when 2 is added to the first part, 2 is subtracted from the second part, 2 is multiplied by the third part, and the fourth part is divided by 2. All the four results should be the same number.

A Problem of Probability

This happened when I was visiting Bagaio, a holiday resort in the Phillippines.

I was lunching with a young mathematics professor who was also holidaying. We were seated at a table by the window. We spoke about various things and finally we hit upon the subject of the determinational of the probability of a coincidence.

The professor, incidentally his name is Prof. Alfredo Garcia — he took out a coin and said 'Now watch, I am going to flip this coin on the table without looking. Tell me what's the probability of a tail-up turn?'

At that time two other friends of ours walked in and joined us at the table for coffee. We briefly explained to them the topic of our discussion.

'First of all, professor, explain to us what is 'probability' said one of the two friends.'

'Yes, please do. Not everyone knows it' I said.

'Certainly. Well it's really very simple. If I toss a coin in the air, there are only two possible ways in which it would fall. Head or tail. Of these only one will be exactly what we want. Let's call it a favourable occurrence. Then it can be deduced mathematically this way.

The number of favourable occurrence = 1
The number of possible occurrence   = 2

In this way the probability of a tail-up can be represented by the fraction ½.

What if it is not a coin.... say it is something more complicated' interrupted one of the friends.

'Say for example a die' joined in the other.

'Yeah, a die. Let me see.... of course.... it's cubical in shape'.

The professor was thoughtful for a moment. Then he continued 'Yeah . . . . it has numbers on each of its faces . . . . 1,2,3,4,5,6, ...'

'Now what's the probability . . . . of . . . . say number 6 turning up'? I asked.

'Well, there are six faces. Therefore we have to see how many possible occurrences there are said the professor. 'Any of the numbers from 1 to 6 can turn up. The favourable occurrence for us, naturally will be 6. And naturally the probability in this case will be 1/6'.

'But can you really compute in this manner any event'? queried one of the friends. 'Take for example, if I were to bet that the very next person to pass our window will be a woman, what's the probability that I would win the bet?'

'Well, I would say it is ½, provided we decide to regard even a little boy as a man and a little girl as a woman', the professor replied.

'That's assuming that there's an equal number of men and women in the world' I joined in.

'In such a case what's the probability that the first wo persons passing the window will be men?' one of the friends asked.

'Well, a computation of this kind will be a little more complicated. We'll have to try all the possible combinations. The first possibility will be that both the persons will be men. Second possibility that the first person may be a man and second a woman. Third, the first person may be a woman and second a man. Fourth, both the persons may be women. That makes four combinations. And of course, of these four combinations only one is favourable'.

'I see' I agreed.

'So, the probability is ¼ the professor continued. 'And that's the solution to your problem'.

We were all silent for a moment. Then one of the friends spoke.

'Supposing, instead of two, we think of three men. What would be the probability that the first three persons to pass our window will be men?'

'The solution is obvious, isn't it?' the professor said. 'We start by computing the number of possible combinations. When we calculated for two passers by, the number of combinations we found was 4. Now by adding one more passer-by we have to double the number of possible combinations, because each of the four groups of the two passers-by can be joined by a man or a woman. That makes the number of possible combinations in this case 4x2 = 8.'

'One would have never thought of it that way' remarked a friend.

'But you see it for a fact! The probability is quiet obvious — it is 1/8. Only one in eight will be a favourable occurrence. The method of calculating the probability is very easy really'.

The professor took out a ball pen from his pocket and wrote on the white table cloth.

'Two passers by, the probability is ½ x ½ = ¼ OK'

'Yes' I agreed.

'For three it is $1/2 \times 1/2 \times 1/2 = 1/8$'

'Agreed' said a friend.

'Now for four the probability will be, naturally, the product of 4 halves, that is 1/16'.

'It appears the probability grows less each time' remarked a friend.

'Right. Take the case of ten passers by, for example. The answers will be the product of 10 halves. Do you know how much it is 1/1024'.

'No' we all said in a chorus.

'In other words' said one of the friends 'If I bet a dollar that the first ten passers-by will be all men, chances of winning the bet is only 1/1024'

'Well I can put up a bet for a $ 100.00 that it will not happen'. The professor said very confidently.

'I can surely use a hundred dollars. Wish I could catch you on that bet professor' I joined.

'But then your chance to win will be only one in one thousand twenty-four'.

'I don't mind . . . . all I would be losing is only $ 1.00'

'Still a dollar is dollar' said a friend.

'And your chances of winning the bet is so remote' said the other.

I looked out of the window. The road was somewhat deserted. After lunch, most people were home enjoying their after-lunch siestas. I looked at my watch. It was almost approaching 2 P.M. — only a minute or so left. I spoke quickly.

'Tell me professor, what are the chances of my winning. If I were to bet one dollar against one hundred that the next hundred passers-by outside our window will be men'.

'Your chances of winning would be even less than one in a million for twenty passers-by and for 100 passers-by the probability would be even less than' he wrote on the table cloth

$$\frac{1}{1000\ 000\ 000\ 000\ 000\ 000\ 000\ 000\ 000\ 000}$$

'Really!' I remarked 'I still want to take the bet with you that the next one hundred passers-by will be men'.

'I will give you one thousand dollars instead of one hundred. You can't win the bet' he said excitedly.

I looked at my watch again. It was only a few seconds before 2 P.M.

As our friends watched us with utter amusement I reached for the professor's hand and shook it, confirming the bet. The very next moment something happend.

In exactly five minutes after that the professor was heading towards the bank to encash all his travellers cheques in order to pay me my one thousand dollars.

How do you think I won my bet.

123

Arrange the Digits

1, 2, 3, 4, 5, 6, 7, 8, 9

Here are the nine digits.

Can you arrange the nine digits in order from left to right and + or — signs only so as to produce a result of 100?

124

Something in the Way of Calculus

We have a rectangular sheet of tinfoil whose dimensions are 32 centimetres by 20 centimetres. Equal squares are cut out at each of the corners.

Can you find the maximum volume of a wooden box which can be lined by suitably bending the tinfoil to cover the base and sides of the box?

125

The Problem of the Music Concert

Recently I was at a music concert in Calcutta. I was sitting only one hundred feet away from the musicians.

The performance was being broadcasted. My sister Vasantha who lives in Bangalore also heard the same concert on the radio. I am sure you know that Bangalore is over a thousand miles away from

Calcutta, and also that sound travels at 1100 feet per second.

Do you think there was any difference in the times at which the music was heard by Vasantha and myself? If so which one of us did hear the given note first?

126

Count the Triangles

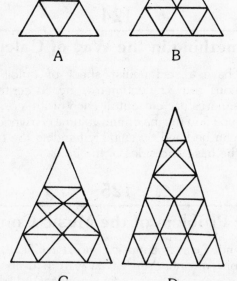

Can you tell how many triangles are there in each of these figures?

Third Dimension of a Box

I have a box. The two dimensions of the box are 4"
and 3". Compute the third dimension of the box so
that the space diagonal of the box is an integer.

128

Out in the Cold

Mammu and I, we were on a tour of West Germany.
It was a very cold winter evening. We stepped in the
street to walk to a coffee shop. Mammu is only five and
a half years old. We were dressed similarly. Who do
you think felt colder?

129

Height of a Room

Given the floor area of a room as 24 feet by 48 feet,
and the space diagonal of the room as 56 feet, can you
find the height of the room?

130

Average Speed

It was a long drive. I drove 60 kilometres at 30
kilometres per hour and then an additional 60
kilometres at 50 kilometres per hour.

Compute my average speed over the 120 kilometres.

131

Special Number

What is special about this number 1729 —?

132

A Problem of Water Lillies

In India water lillies grow extremely rapidly in the ponds. If the growth enlarged so much that each day it covered a surface double that which it filled the day before, so that at the end of the 20th day if entirely covered the pond, in which it **grew**, how long would it take two water lillies of the same size at the outset and at the same rate of growth to cover the same pond?

133

Decode the Mnemonic

Here is a piece of Mnemonic:
>   Now I — even I, would celebrate
>   In rhymes unapt the great
>   Immortal syracusan rivaled never more,
>   who in his wondrous lore
>   Passed on before,
>   Left men his guidance
>   How to circles mensurate.
Can you tell what it signifies?

134

Computing to Infinity

How much is
$$1/7 + 2/7^2 + 1/7^3 + 2/7^4 + 1/7^5 + 2/7^6 + 1/7^7 \ldots.$$
$$\text{to infinity ?}$$

135

How to Increase the Volume?

A cylindrical container has a radius of eight inches and a height of three inches.

Compute how many inches should be added to either the radius or height to give the same increase in the volume?

136

A Problem of Family Relations

Every man or woman alive today had 2 parents, 4 grand-parents, 8 great-grand parents, 16 great-great-grand parents, 32 great, great, great grand parents and so on.

Let us take the case of Ram. Two generations ago Ram had 2 x 2 or 2^2, or 4 ancestors. Three generations ago he had 2 x 2 x 2 or 2^3 or 8 ancestors. Four generations ago he had 2 x 2 x 2 x2 or 2^4 or 16 ancestors.

Assuming that there are 20 years to a generation, can you tell 400 years back how many ancestors did Ram have?

137

Counting A Billion

If you were to count one number per second and counted seven hours per day, how long would it take you to count to a Billion?

138

A Question of Identity

Is this a prime number?
1000009

139

Deck of Cards

A standard deck of cards has 52 cards. What is the probability that six cards drawn at random will all be black cards?

140

Value of 'X'

17 . x = 17 + x

What is the value of X ?

141

Solving Problems

Romila appeared for a maths exam. She was given 100 problems to solve. She tried to solve all of them correctly but some of them went wrong. Any how she scored 85.

Her score was calculated by subtracting two times the number of wrong answers from the number of correct answers.

Can you tell how many problems she solved correctly?

142

Boy or Girl

Vikram Chadda has two children, and at least one of them is a girl. What is the probability that both children are girls?

143

Playing Children

A group of boys and girls are playing. 15 boys leave. There remain two girls for each boy. Then 45 girls leave. There remain five boys for each girl. How many boys were in the original group?

144

Amicable Numbers

The numbers 220 and 284 are known as amicable numbers. The reason is the sum of the proper divisions of 220 equals 284 and what is even more interesting is the sum of the proper divisors of 284 equals 220.

So far about 100 pairs of amicable numbers are known. Can you find some in four digits?

145

Matching Pair of Socks

Mammu has 16 pairs of white socks and 16 pairs of brown socks. She keeps them all in the same drawer. If she picks out three socks at random what is the probability she will get a matching pair?

146

Naming A Number

Take a good look at this number: 222221
Is it a prime number?

147

A Problem of Roofing Paper

For doing the interior decorations of my apartment,

I have bought a roll of roofing paper. I do not know its exact thickness, but let us assume it is X. How can I find out how long the roll is without unrolling it? In other words, can you derive a formula for length of roll if the radius is r?

148

Positive Integers

What are the three positive integers whose sum is 43 and the sum of the cubes of the three integers is 17299^2.

149

Dimensions of a Rectangle

Only two rectangles have dimensions that are integers and their area and perimeter equal the same number. Can you find both?

150

My Bank Balance

My bank pays me 4% simple interest compounded annually. If I deposit one hundred dollars at the beginning of each year for five years, what would be my balance at the end of five years?

151

The Benediktov Problem

The great Russian poet Benediktov (1807-1873) was

very fond of mathematics and he collected and compiled a whole volume of tricky brain teasers. Though his work was never published, the manuscript was found in 1924. An interesting problem contained in the manuscript, captioned 'An Ingenious Way of Solving a Tricky Problem' goes as follows:

One woman who made a living by selling eggs had 90 eggs which she wanted to sell, so she sent her three daughters to the market, giving 10 eggs to her eldest and cleverest daughter, 30 to the second and 50 to the third.

'You'd better agree among yourselves,' she told them, 'about the price you're going to ask for the eggs, and keep to it. Stick to the price you decide upon. But I hope that, in spite of your agreement, the eldest, being the cleverest, will receive as much for her ten eggs as the second will receive for her thirty and will teach the second to sell her thirty eggs for as much as the youngest will sell her fifty. In other words, each of you is to bring home the same amount, and the total for the 90 eggs is not to be less than 90 kopeks.'

A kopek may be treated as a rupee. How do you think the girls carried out the instructions of their mother.

152

A Computing Problem

Compute:
(100-1) (100-2) (100-3) .... (100+1) (100+2) (100 + 3) = ?

153

Number Wheel

Here is a number wheel. Can you arrange the

numbers 1 to 9 in such a way as to have one of them in the centre and the rest at the ends of the diameters?

The sum of the three numbers on each diameter should be 15.

154

Largest Number

What is the largest number you can write with the following Roman numerals?

I. C. X V.L.

You can use each numeral only once.

155

A Circle and a Triangle

What do you call a circle which passes through the vertices of a triangle?

156

Every One has the Same Answer!

We were a group of four, sipping coffee in a wayside cafe near Montmartre in Paris. Andre is a student of mathematics at the University and he is very clever with numbers. He showed us a very interesting puzzle.

He asked us all to think of a number — any single digit. We were not supposed to disclose the number to each other. He asked us to add 9 to the number and then square it. From this he asked us to subtract the square of the original number and again subtract 61 from the result. This number, he asked us to multiply by 2, add 24 and subtract 36 times the original number. Now he asked us to take the square root of that number.

To our surprise he told us the exact number we had finally got and what was even more amazing was that we, all the three of us, had got the same final result.

How do you explain it?

157

A Circle and a Polygon

What do you call a circle that touches all the sides of a polygon ?

159

Life of the Sun

Can you tell how long the sun has existed?

159

Number of Poles in a Fence

A farmer built a fence around his 17 cows, in a square shaped region. He used 27 fence poles on each side of the square.

How many poles did he need altogether?

160

A Problem of Population

If human beings did not die the earth would sooner or later be overcrowded with the progeny of just one couple. If death did not hinder the growth of human life, within a score of years or so our continents would be teaming with millions of people fighting each other for living space.

Let us take for instance the case of two couples today. Supposing each of these couple give birth to 4 children and the eight children in turn form 4 couples and each couple in turn give birth to 4 children, and those 16 children again form eight couples and give birth to 4 children each and so on, can you tell exactly the number of progeny the two initial couples would have after 10 generations?

161

A Mule and a Donkey Eating Wheat

This following problem is supposed to have been given by Euclid in his lectures in Alexandria about 280 B.C.

A mule and donkey were going to the market laden

with wheat. The mule said "if you give me one measure, I should carry twice as much as you, but if I give you one, we should have equal burdens."

What were their burdens?

162

Age of Our Earth

Can you tell how old is our earth approximately?

163

Crossing Circles

What do you call two circles which cut 'right' across each other?

164

Weight of Sugar

Can you tell what is heavier—a cup of lump sugar or a cup of powdered sugar?

165

Find out the Numbers

The difference between two numbers is 54. They are composed of the same two digits reversed. What are the numbers?

166

Weight and Height

There are two men. One is tall and the other is a midget. The tall man is two metres in height and the midget stands 1 metre high. By how much does the tall man outweigh the midget?

167

Six Rows of Children

24 children are attending a flag hoisting ceremony. How can you arrange them in six rows with each row comprising 5.

168

Magic Star

Here is an eight pointed star.
Can you fill in the circles at the points of intersection with numbers from 1 to 16 so that the total adds upto 34 on each side of the square and 34 at the vertices?

169

Switching Problem

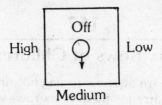

Here is a light switch. Please note the order of the positions. If the light is now at medium and it is switched 3922 times what will be the position of the switch?

170

A Steamer's Route

A 150 metre long steamer has changed its direction through 30 degrees while moving through a distance equal to twice its own length. Can you tell the radius in the circle in which it moved?

171

Continue the Sequence

What are the next two terms in the sequence?
1/5, 0, 1, –2, 9, –28, 101 ....

172

Square of a Natural Number

Can you name the square of a natural number that is twice the square of some other natural number?

173

Find Numbers

12 and 21 are numerical reversals of each other; so are the squares of these numbers; 144 and 441. How many more numbers can you think of which have this property?

174

Absolute Value

Supposing the roots of a quadratic equation are: 8/5 and –7/3
What is the absolute value of the coefficient of the x term, if the equation is written in standard form $(ax^2 + bx + c = 0)$, and $a = 1$

175

Water Pipes

A circular pipe with an inside diameter of six feet can carry a certain amount of water

How many circular pipes with an inside diameter of one inch will be needed to carry the same amout of water?

176

Broken Eggs

A boy was carrying a basket of eggs. He fell down and all the eggs broke. When he went back home without any eggs his mother asked how many he had been carrying altogether in the basket. He was unable to remember.

But he was able to recall that when they were counted two at a time one was left, when counted three at a time one was left, when counted four at a time one was left, when counted five at a time none were left.

Can you tell how many eggs were broken.

177

Volume of the New Bottle

If all the dimensions of a one litre bottle are doubled what is the volume of the new bottle?

178

A Dinner Party

At a dinner party every two guests used a dish of rice between them. Every three guests used a dish of *dhal* and every four used a dish of meat between them. There were altogether 65 dishes.

How many guests were present?

Triangles in a Star

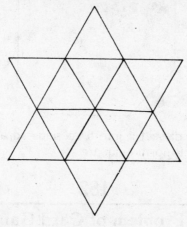

How many triangles are there (any size) in this figure?

Brothers and Sisters

In the Sareen family each daughter has the same number of brothers as she has sisters and each son has twice as many sisters as he has brothers. Now can you tell me how many sons and how many daughters do the Sareen family have?

Dissection of an Octagon

Here is an octagon

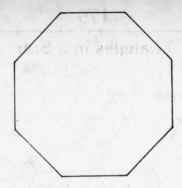

Can you dissect it into 5 sections so as it can be rearranged to form a square.

182

A Problem of Card Game

Asha and I were playing cards. The stake was 1 P a game. At the end I had won three games and Asha had won three Paises. How many games did we play?

183

Squaring the Circle

What is meant by squaring the circles?

184

Building a Play House

Rakesh and Nikhilesh were carrying pieces of timber to build a playhouse. Nikhilesh said to Rakesh 'Give me one of your pieces so that we shall both be carrying the same number of pieces'.

'No' said Rakesh, proudly wanting to display his strength 'Give me one of yours and I shall be carrying twice your weight'.

Can you tell how many pieces of timber were each Rakesh and Nikhilesh carrying?

185

Missing Letters

Here is a logical pattern:
O. T. T. F. F. S. S. E. N
What are the next nine letters?

186

Selling Eggs

The egg vendor calls on his first customer and sells half his eggs and half an egg. To the second customer he sells half of what he had left and half an egg, and to the third customer he sells half of what he had then left and half an egg. By the way he did not break any eggs. In the end three eggs were remaining.

How many did he start out with?

187

Guess the Missing Number

Here is a multiplication
7451 x 3982 = 29 * 69882
One digit is missing from the product. Can you find the missing number without performing the multiplication?

Width of the Human Hair

It is estimated that the width of the human hair is $\dfrac{3}{1000}$ inch

About how many hairs placed side by side would measure an inch?

189

Span of Life

Can you tell how old is life on our Earth?

190

Consecutive Natural Numbers

There are two consecutive natural numbers whose product is equal to the product of three consecutive natural numbers for example (x + 1) = y (y + 1) (y + 2).What are the two numbers?

191

Speed of Ships

What is the standard measurement of the speed of ships?

192

Size of a Cherry

The cherry is a round fruit with a round stone. If the
flesh of the cherry around the stone is as thick as the
stone itself, can you calculate mentally how much
more pulp than stone there is in the cherry?

193

Stolen Mangoes

Three naughty boys stole some mangoes from a
garden. As it was late in the evening, they decided to
divide the fruit equally among them in the morning,
and went to sleep.

At night while the other two were sleeping, one boy
woke up, tip-toed to the basket of mangoes, counted
them and ate one. From the remainder he took a
precise third and went back to sleep.

After some time a second boy woke up. He counted
the mangoes, ate one, took an exact third of the
remaining and went back to sleep.

A little before sun rise the third boy also woke up,
ate one, and like the other two boys took a precise
third of the remainder in whole mangoes.

In the morning, all the three boys went together to
the basket of mangoes, counted them. Amongst them
they found one which was over ripe—almost rotten.
They threw it away. From the remainder they made an
exact division.

How many mangoes in all did they steal?

194

Computing to Infinity

What is the sum to infinity?
$s = 1 + (-1) + 1 + (-1) + (-1) + (-1) + (-1) + 1 + ...$

195

Factors

Compute the number
$n(n^2 + 1)(n^2 - 1)$
If n = 1, 2, 3, 4, 5, 6, 7, 8, 17.
When 'n' is an integer greater than 1 what factors do all the numbers possess?

196

Missing Digit

A three digit number consists of 9,5 and one more number. When these digits are reversed and then subtracted from the original number the answer yielded will be consisting of the same digits arranged yet in a different order. What is the other digit?

197

A Jumping Frog

A frog starts climbing a 30 ft wall. Each hour he climbs 3 ft and slips back 2. How many days does it take him to reach the top and get out?

Vanishing one Rupee

Two farmer's wives set out to the market to sell some oranges. Each had 30 oranges for sale. The first sold hers at 2 a rupee and the other at 3 a rupee. When all the oranges were sold the former had made in all Rs. 15 and the latter Rs. 10, a total of Rs. 25.

The next day when they set out for the market, they decided to do business together. So they pooled their sixty oranges and sold them at the rate of 5 for Rs 2 (Two a rupee plus three a rupee).

But when the oranges were all sold out and they counted their takings, to their dismay, they found that they had only Rs 24 in all. They could not understand where the other one rupee went.

They ended up accusing each other of having appropriated the rupee.

Where did the one rupee go?

199

Add the Numbers

Find the value of:

CXVI + XIII + VI + CCLXV

200

A Three Digital Problem

By using only the digits 9, 9, 9, can you make:
a) 1, b) 4, c) 6? You can adopt mathematical processes such as + , −, x, ÷, $\sqrt{}$ etc.

201

Smallest Number

What is the smallest number which when divided by 10 leaves a remainder of 9, when divided by 9 leaves a remainder of 8, when divided by 8 leaves a remainder of 7 and so on until when divided by 2 leaves a remainder of 1?

202

Fast and Slow Running Train

An express train leaves Calcutta for Bombay at the same time as a passenger train leaves Bombay for Calcutta. The express travels at the speed of 60 kilometres per hour and the slow train at the rate of 30 kilometres per hour. Which is further from Calcutta when they meet?

203

Earth and the Sun

What is the distance between earth and the sun?

204

Red Corpuscles

The cubic inch of average human blood is said to contain eighty thousand million red corpuscles. If an average adult has 210 cubic inches blood, how many red corpuscles are there in the body of an adult?

205

A Global View

Do you know the surface area of the globe, counting all continents and oceans?

206

Price of a Bottle

A bottle and its cork together cost Rs. 1.10, and the bottle costs Re 1 more than its cork. What is the price of the bottle?

207

A Special Magic Square

Here is a magic square. Can you tell what is special about it?

96	11	89	68
88	69	91	16
61	86	18	99
19	98	66	81

208

A Cipher

What is a 'Cipher'?

Piling up Corpuscles

The red corpuscles in the human body are said to have a thickness of .00008 inch. Approximately how high would all the corpuscles in an average adult's body be if they could be piled on top of one another without compression?

210

A Book Worm's Route

There are three volumes of the same book each three centimetres thick. They are kept in shelf side by side in order. Volume I, II and III. If a book worm starts outside the front cover of volume I and eats its way through to the outside of the back cover of volume III, travelling in a straight line, how far does it travel?

211

Share of a Garden

My friend owns a small rose garden in Bangalore. My sister Lalitha has a share of 3/5 of it, and my sister Vasantha has twice as much as myself. What fraction of the field belongs to me?

212

A Problem of Wearing Shoes

On a certain island, 5% of the 10000 inhabitants are one legged and half of the others go barefoot. What is the least number of shoes needed in the island?

A Problem of being Photographed

My friend Asha, Neesha, Vijay, Parveen and Seema and myself, we decided to have a group photo taken in the studio. We decided to sit in a row. How many different arrangements can be made of the order in which we could have sat?

After the sitting at the photo studio, we all decided to lunch together in a restaurant.

The waiter led us to a round table. We had a little bit of an argument about who should sit next to whom.

How many different arrangements can be made of the order in which we could have sat?

214

The Three Integers

What are the three integers in arithmetic sequence whose product is prime?

215

A Bigger Dozen

Six dozen dozen: is it greater than, equal to, or less than half a dozen dozen?

216

Smallest Integer

$7! < 10^7$ $8! < 10^8$

Which is the smallest integer S so that $S! > 10^s$

Match Sticks Game

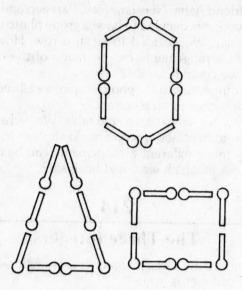

Here are three different figures made out of 8 match sticks. They are all different in size. What would be the biggest possible figure you can make out of these eight match sticks?

218

Selecting a Candidate

A school announced the opening of the posts for six teachers in the local newspaper. 12 persons applied for the job. Can you tell in how many different ways this selection can be made?

219

A Batting Problem

A team has nine players. How many possible batting orders are there?

220

Smallest Integer

?..M

If the largest of x consecutive integers is M, what is the smallest?

221

The Fly and the Molasses

A cylindrical glass container is 20 centimetres tall and has a diameter of 10 centimetres. On the inside wall, three centimetres from the upper circular base, there is a drop of molasses. On the lateral surface, diametrically opposite it, there is a fly.

Which is the shortest route for the fly to take to reach the molasses?

222

A Set of Bat and Ball

Mammu wanted a bat very badly to play with her ball. The shopkeeper showed me a set of bat and ball. He told me that they would together cost me Rs. 3.75. But I did not need the ball as Mammu had one already.

Then he said that the bat would cost me 75 Paise more than the ball.

What was the cost of the bat and the ball?

223

Edges of a Pencil

How many edges has a hexagonal pencil?

224

The 'Lattice' Method

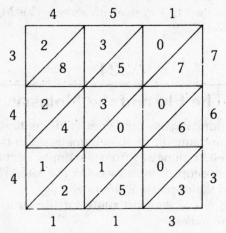

This is the multiplication of the numbers 451 x 763. The 'Lattice' method has been used.

Can you find the product and the method?

225

The Television Tower

Bombay has a high television tower. Supposing you do not know the height, but you have a photograph of the tower, is there any way in which you can find the real height of the tower?

226

Football Game

In order to ensure that one forecast is correct, how many different forecasts must be made of 5 football games?

227

Factorials

There are many factorials that can be expressed as the product of two or more other factorials. To give you an example:

7! x 6! = 10!

How many others can you find?

228

Open Pantograph

What is the geometrical shape associated with an open pantograph?

229

A Chess Board

A regular chess board has 8 by 8 squares. How many individual rectangles can you identify?

230

Rising Tide

The ship was sailing. The tide was rising at the rate of 16 inches per hour. Four rungs were already below the water. Each rung was 1½ inches thick and there was a gap of eight inches between rungs.

After five and one half hours later how many rungs of the ladder would have been submerged?

231

The Weight of a Pan

Two pans are similar in shape. They are also of the same thickness. However one of them is eight times more capacious than the other.

Can you tell how heavier is the bigger one than the other?

232

A Boat Race

The yacht club recently held a boat race. The captain had some difficulty deciding the order of rowing in the boat for his crew.

3 of his crew were strokeside oarsmen only and 2 of them were bow side oarsmen only. Weights and personal preferences were not important really.

In how many ways the captain could have arranged his eight men to form the crew?

233

Giving Away Five Billion Rupees

Supposing you had five billion rupees and you gave away a Rs.500 note every minute, how long would it take you to give away all your money?

234

Two Excellent Mnemonics

'To disrupt a playroom is commonly a practise of children'

AND

'It enables a numskull to memorize quality of numerals!

These two pieces of mnemonics signify a certain mathematical term to 9 places of decimals.

What is the term?

235

A Problem of Flies

The common fly is considered an appallingly prolific insect. Each female fly is capable of laying 120 eggs at a time. Out of the eggs hatched, half of them are generally females.

The female flies hatched grow sufficiently within 20 days to lay eggs themselves.

Assuming that the female fly lays her first eggs on the 1st of April, can you tell how many eggs will be hatched in the course of that summer, in the seventh generation.

236

Height of a Palm Tree

A palm tree was 90 cm high, when it was planted. It grows by an equal number of cms each year, and at the end of the seventh year it was one ninth taller than at the end of the sixth year. Can you tell how tall was the tree at the end of the twelfth year?

237

Make a Series

What are the next three terms to the series:
1 + 3 + 7 + 15 + 31 + 63 + ...

238

Around the Equator

Supposing one decides to walk around the earth on the equator, the top of the person's head would describe a circle whose circumference would be longer than the circle described by his feet.

How great do you think the difference would be?

239

Intersecting Squares

There are two squares. One is large and the other one is small. The large square has a side of 17 units and the smaller square has a side of 15 units with its vertex at the centre of the large square, and intersects the side of the large square 3½ units from the vertex.

What is the area of the shaded overlapping region?

94

240

Weight of Diamonds

What is the measure used to weigh diamonds?

241

Meaning of the Term

What does the term 'Casting out the nines' refer to?

242

Make a Sequence

What are the next two terms of the sequence?
1, 1, 5, 17, 61, 217 ....

243

Natural Numbers

Using the numeral 4 just four times only combining it with any mathematical symbols + , –, x, $\sqrt{\ }$

Can you form each of these natural numbers 1, 2, 3, 4, 5, 6, 7, 8, 9, 10, 12, 14, 15, 16, 17, 18, 19 and 20.

244

The Spoilt Holiday

A group of friends and myself went on a holiday to a hill station. It rained for 13 days. But when it rained in the morning the afternoon was lovely. And when it rained in the afternoon the day was preceded by a clear morning.

Altogether there were 11 very nice mornings and 12 very nice afternoons. How many days did our holiday last?

245

A Problem of Drinks

I love to mix drinks. When I have one glass orangeade and one glass lemonade each glass contains the same amount. I take 2 ounces full of the orangeade and mix it with the lemonade, and then I take 2 ounces full of this mixture and put it back in the orangeade. What do you think of the resulting mixture?

Do you think there is more orangeade in the lemonade or more lemonade in the orangeade?

246

A Simple Problem

Simplify:

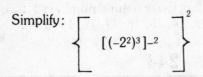

$$\left\{ \left[(-2^2)^3 \right]^{-2} \right\}^2$$

247

Googolplex

How much is a googolplex?

248

Tell the Time

Can you tell at what time between 7 and 8 O'clock, the two hands of a clock, will be in a straight line?

249

Name of the Line

What is the name of the line referred to when you say
'Cut a circle in two points'?

250

A Cardioid

What is a cardioid?

251

A Problem of Age

Today was Lakshmi's birthday. She turned 24. Lakshmi is twice as old as Ramu was when Lakshmi was as old as Ramu now. How old is Ramu now?

252

The Common Name

What is the common name for a regular hexahedron?

Name the Circle

Can you name the circle which is implied by 'The circle which touches all sides of a polygon'.

254

Find out the Value

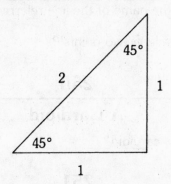

Can you tell the value of the following:

Sin 45° =   Cot 45° =

Cos 45° =   Sec 45° =

Tan 45° =   Csc 45° =

255

Alter the Numbers

Here is a circle with marked numbers. Can you alter the numbers so that the sum of any two adjacent numbers is equal to the sum of the pair of numbers at the other ends of the diameters.

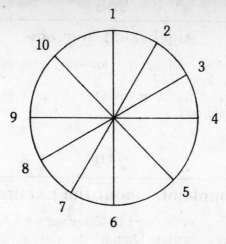

256

Climbing Problem of Creepers

Two creepers, one jasmine and the other rose, are both climbing up and round a cylindrical tree trunk. The jasmine twists clockwise and the rose anti-clockwise, and they both start at the same point on the ground. Before they reach the first branch on the tree the jasmine has made 5 complete twists and the rose 3 twists. Not counting the bottom and the top, how many times do they cross?

257

Throwing the Dice

We have two dice one red and one black. In how many different ways can they be thrown?

Algebraic Language

Can you change the following statement into algebraic language?

'A certain number is equal to twice another number diminished by 5'.

259

Complaints about the Excursion

Our group consisted of 400 when we went on an overseas excursion. On our return we were asked if we had any complaints to make. 240 had no complaints at all. Amongst rest 60 complained about the delays everywhere, 3 complained about the delays, food, and lack of facilities, 11 about food and lack of facilities, 8 about delays and food, and 7 about delays and lack of facilities. An equal number complained about either lack of facilities or food only.

How can you represent these figures on a venn diagram and calculate the number of persons who complained about the food only?

260

Insert Numbers in Circles

Can you arrange the numbers 1, 2, 3, 4, 5, 6, 7, 8, 9, 10, 11 and 12 in the twelve circles of their figure so that the sum of the three numbers on each of the six sides is the same, and the three circles connected by single line and the two circles connected by the double line also give the same sum?

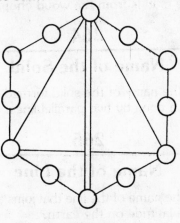

261

One Word Answer

Can you tell in one word the name of the following suffix?

'The medians of a triangle have this point in common'.

262

Simpson's Rule

To what use is Simpson's rule put?'

263

Sound of a Striking Axe

Sound is said to travel in air at about 1100 feet per

second. A man hears the axe strike the tree 11/5 seconds after he sees it strike the tree. How far would you say the man is from the wood chopper?

264

Name of the Solid

What is the name of the solid formed by cutting a pyramid or a cone by two parallel lines.

265

Name of the Line

What is the name of the line that joins all the points of the same latitude on the earth?

266

A Problem of Eggs

A farmer has six baskets full of chicken and duck eggs he is taking to the market to sell. Basket A has 29 eggs, basket B has 14 eggs, basket C has 23 eggs, basket D has 6 eggs, basket E has 5 eggs and basket F has 12 eggs.

The farmer points to a particular basket and says 'If I sell all the eggs in this basket, I shall have twice as many chicken eggs left as duck eggs.'

Which was the basket he was pointing at?

267

Value of K

If $K = a - b^{a-b}$ what is the value of K when $a = -1$ and $b = -2$?

268

Honey Comb

What particular geometrical shape do you associate with the cell in a honey comb.

269

Sides of a Triangle

The sides of a right–angled triangle have a length of an exact number of m. Supposing the perpendicular is 9m long and the hypotonuse is 1m longer than the base, what is the length of the sides?

270

Name the Triangle

What is the name of the triangle formed by joining the facet of the perpendiculars from the vertices of a triangle to the opposite side?

271

Playing Chess

A chess board has 64 squares. In how many different positions can you arrange two draughts on the board?

272

Rows of Numerals

Name the triangle which does not have three lines for sides but only rows of numerals.

Count the Faces

Can you tell how many faces does a stellated Dodecahedron have?

274

Problem of a Handbag

I found a very nice handbag in the shop that I thought I should simply must have. The price was Rs. 10. But I did not have the Rs. 10.

The storekeeper was known to me. He said that he had a credit system by which I could pay Re. 1 only at the time of purchase and the balance Rs 10 could be paid by me at the rate of Re 1 per week for 10 weeks.

Can you tell what annual rate of interest the storekeeper was charging me?

275

A Broken Gold Chain

A goldsmith was given a chain to be repaired. The chain was torn into five equal sections of three links each.

The goldsmith began to wonder how many links he would have to open up and then solder. After some thinking he decided that it would be four.

What do you think? Could he have done this job with opening up a fewer links and then soldered?

276

Quick Descent

What does the curve of quick descent refer to?

277

Square Number

Can you prove that the sum of two adjacent triangular numbers is a square number.

278

A Series of Numbers

Can you write 10 numbers from least to greatest which have a remainder of 3 after division by 7. What kind of series is formed and what is the common difference?

279

Length of the Strip

What is the length of the strip of all millimetre squares in one square metre, if placed one along side the other?

You must calculate mentally.

280

Moving a Safe

A heavy safe is to be moved. Two cylindrical steel bars of diameter 7 centimetres are used as rollers.

When the rollers have made one revolution, how far will the safe have moved forward?

281

Filling Wine in Barrels

A friend of mine in London has a very nice cellar. He has two large barrels in the cellar. The larger barrel is mostly empty. But the smaller barrel is only 5/6th full of wine while it can hold 536 litres.

Supposing he empties the smaller barrel and fills the bigger barrel to find that the wine fills only 4/9ths of it, how much wine would the larger barrel hold when full?

282

A Standing Tripod

Why is it that a tripod stands firmly, even when its three legs are of different length?

283

Women at Club Socials

Women outnumbered men by 16 at a club social. Sometimes the number of women exceeds nine times the number of men by 32. What was the number of men and women at the club?

284

Constellation Pegasus

What particular geometrical shape is associated with Constellation Pegasus?

285

A Game of Billiards

Rajiv, Sanjiv and Vijay were playing a game of billiards. Rajiv can give Sanjiv 10 points in 50, and Sanjiv can give Vijay 10 points in 50. How many points in 50 must Rajiv give Sanjiv to make an even game?

286

Finding a Way

Here is the plan of an estate. It has been divided into square lots. There are many ways a person can take to reach from point A to point B. Can you tell how many different ways of the same length are there for a person to take?

Playing a Record

A gramophone record has a diameter of 30.5 centimetres. The centre is unused and has a diameter of 10 centimetres. There is also a smooth outer edge 1.25 centimetres wide around the recording.

If the grooves are 36 to the centimetre, how far does the needle move during the actual playing of the record?

288

Greatest and the Least

Can you name the greatest and the least of the following?

$\log(2+4)$, $(\log 2 + \log 4)$, $\log(6-3)$ and $(\log 6 - \log 3)$.

289

Sum of Odd Numbers

Find the sum of the first 70 odd numbers.

290

Length of a Train

A train is travelling at the speed of 96 kilometres per hour. It takes 3 seconds to enter a tunnel and 30 seconds more to pass through it completely. What is the length of the train and the tunnel?

Planting Trees

If you wished to plant some trees so that each was equidistant from every other tree, what is the largest number you could plant?

Name of a Sieve

What is 'The Sieve of Erastosthenes'?

Segments and Dots

Here are some dotted points. Can you draw four segments without lifting your pencil off the paper in such a way that each of the points is at least one of the segments?

O   O   O

O   O   O

O   O   O

Value of the Series

Take a good look at the following series:

$$\frac{1}{1} - \frac{1}{3} + \frac{1}{5} - \frac{1}{7} + \frac{1}{9} - \frac{1}{11} + \frac{1}{13} - \frac{1}{15} + \dots$$

Find the values of the series and multiply the answer by 4. You will notice that a well-known value approximates this product. Even more interesting is that as you add more terms the approximation becomes closer.

295

Name of the Exchange

In Great Britain some years back the first three letters of a telephone number used to indicate the name of the exchange. How many such arrangements of 3 letters is it possible to devise from the 26 letters of the alphabet?

296

Filling a Cistern

Pipe S can fill cistern in 2 hours and pipe K can fill a cistern in 3 hours. Pipe Y can empty it in 5 hours. Supposing all the pipes are turned on when the cistern is completely empty, how long will it take to fill?

297

A Thirst Problem

Rajiv and Sanjiv went camping. They took their own water in big plastic bottles.

Rajiv got thirsty and drank half the water in his bottle. A little later on he drank 1/3 of what was left. Some time afterwards he drank 1/4 of what remained and so on.

Sanjiv also had a bottle of the same size. He drank

half the bottle at the first instance, half of what remained when he drank next and so on.

After each took ten drinks, the water Rajiv had left was how many times greater than the water Sanjiv had left?

298

Snapping a Plane

A plane has a span of 12 metres. It was photographed as it was flying directly overhead with a camera with a depth of 12 cm.

In the photo the span of the plane was 8 mm.

Can you tell how high was the plane when it was snapped?

299

A Running Race

Rajiv, Sanjiv and Vijay join a running race. The distance is 1500 metres. Rajiv beats Sanjiv by 30 metres and Vijay by 100 metres. By how much could Sanjiv beat Vijay over the full distance if they both ran as before?

300

An Election Problem

My club had a problem recently. They had to appoint a Secretary from among the men and a Joint Secretary from among the women.

We have a membership of 12 men and 10 women. In how many ways can the selection be made?

Flying Around

This happened in the Heathrow airport, London. I had just missed a flight. So I decided to kill some time in the Cafetaria until my next flight was ready.

A man walked in and asked my permission to join me at my table.

Sipping coffee we began to chat. He told me he was a commercial pilot and in the course of his work he has flown all over the world. I also gathered that he was a Russian. He posed this very interesting puzzle to me:

'One fine day I just decided to fly around—no fixed destination—just fly around. I took away from Leningrad in a northerly direction. I flew continuously for five hundred kilometres. Then I turned my direction. I flew eastward 500 kilometres. I turned direction again I turned south and covered another 500 kilometres. Now again I turned my direction. I flew 500 kilometres in the westerly direction and landed. Can you tell me where did I land? West, East, South or North of Leningrad?'

'Oh well' I said quickly 'Leningrad, naturally'.

'No' he said.

'Where else would you possibly land? 500 kilometres north, 500 kilometres east, 500 kilometres south and 500 kilometres west. You are exactly where you started from'.

'Not at all' he said.

'I don't understand!'

'I actually landed in Lake Ladoga'.

'Really! How could that be'.

He explained to me in detail and also drew a sketch to illustrate how he could not have possibly landed back in Leningrad.

What do you think his explanation was?

Solutions

1 Let us assume that originally Meena had X rupees and Y 20 paise coins. Going shopping she had (100 X + 20 Y) paise

She returned with only (100 Y + 20 X) paise.

This last sum, as we know, is one-third of the original and therefore

3(100 Y + 20 X) = 100 X + 20 Y

Simplifying we have X = 7 Y

If Y is 1 then X is 7. Assuming this so Meena had 7.20 rupees when she set out for shopping.

This is wrong because Meena actually had about 15 rupees.

Let us see now what we get if Y = 2. Then X = 14.

The original sum was 14.40 rupees which accords with the condition of the problem.

If we assume that Y = 3 then the sum will be too big — 21.60 rupees.

Therefore the only suitable answer is 14.40 rupees.

After shopping Meena had 2 one rupee notes and 14 twenty Paise coins.

This is actually 1/3rd of the original sum 1,440 : 3 = 480.

Meena's purchases, therefore, cost

14.40 — 4.80 = Rs. 9.60

2 There is nothing to explain here. The driving time there and back is absolutely the same because 90 minutes and 1 hour and 30 minutes are one and the same thing.

This problem is meant for inattentive readers who may think that there is some difference between 90 minutes and 1 hour 30 minutes.

3 The smallest integer that can be written with two digits is not 10 as one may assume. But it is expressed as follows:

$$\frac{1}{1} \frac{2}{2} \frac{3}{3} \ \frac{4}{4} \text{ etc upto } \frac{9}{9}$$

4 It is very easy to answer this question. We can find the number of times all the five groups met on one and the same day in the first quarter — the New Year's excluded — by finding the least common multiple of 2, 3, 4, 5 and 6. This isn't difficult. It is 60.

Therefore, the five will all meet again on the 61st day.

The literary group will meet after 30 two-day intervals, the Dramatic after 20 three-day intervals, the Musical after 15 four-day intervals, the Dancing after 12 five-day intervals, and the Painting after 10 six-day intervals.

In other words, they can meet on the one and same day only once in 60 days. And since there are 90 days in the first quarter, it means there can only be one other day on which they all meet.

Now coming to the second question, this is positively more difficult to find the answer. How many days are there when none of the groups meets in the first quarter?

To find the answer to this, it is necessary to write down all the numbers from 1 to 90 and then strike out all the days when the literary group meets — for example the 1st, 3rd, 5th, 7th, 9th etc.

Then we must cross out the Dramatic Group days — for example 4th, 7th, 10th etc.

This way we must cross out the days of the musical, dancing and painting groups also. Then the numbers that remain are the days when none of the groups meet.

When we do that we will find that there are 24 such days — eight in January (2. 8. 12. 14. 18. 20. 24 and 30), seven in February and nine in March.

5 People often think of the number 1111 as the biggest number that can be written with four 1's. But there is a number many, many times greater than this number, namely : 11^{11}

$11^{11} = 285311670611$

As you can see 11^{11} is almost 250 million times greater than 1111.

6 68 regions. Each new tangent increases the non-enclosed areas by two.

7 This problem can be solved only by application of algebra. Supposing we take X for the years, the age three years hence will be X + 3 and the age three years ago X – 3.

Now we have the equation $3(X + 3) – 3(X – 3) = X$

When we solve this, we obtain : 18. The girl is 18 years old.

To check this: Three years hence she will be 21 and three years ago she was 15.

And the difference is: $(3 \times 21) – (3 \times 15) = 63 – 45 = 18$

8 Since a = b, a – b = 0. Hence division by zero.

9 $(1/8)^{-2/3} = ((1/2)^3)^{-2/3} = (1/2)^{-2} = \frac{1}{(1/2)^2} = \frac{1}{1/4} = 4$

10 There are many ways of solving this problem without equations.

Here is one way :

In five minutes the son covers ¼ of the way and the father $1/6$ i.e. $1/4 - 1/6 = 1/12$ less than the son.

Since the father was $1/6$ of the way ahead of the son, the son would catch up with him after $1/6 : 4/12 = 2$ five minute intervals, or 10 minutes.

There is one other way of doing this calculation which is even simpler:

To get to work the father needs 10 minutes more than the son. If he were to leave home 10 minutes earlier, they would both arrive at work at the same time. If the father were to leave only five minutes earlier, the son would overhaul him half way to work i.e. 10 minutes later, since it takes him 20 minutes to cover the whole distance.

11 One can think of at least 9 examples :

$$39 \times 186 = 7254$$
$$18 \times 297 = 5346$$
$$28 \times 157 = 4396$$
$$42 \times 138 = 5796$$
$$12 \times 483 = 5796$$
$$48 \times 159 = 7632$$
$$4 \times 1738 = 6952$$
$$27 \times 198 = 5346$$
$$4 \times 1963 = 7852$$

If you try patiently, perhaps you may come up with some more.

12 $(2)^{(n)} = 28$; $\dfrac{n(n-1)}{2} = 28$; $\dfrac{n^2 - n}{2} = 28$;

$n^2 - n - 56 = 0$; $n = 8$. There were altogether 8 guests present at the get-together.

116

13 Well one would always think that the small cog wheel will rotate three times. But this is a mistake. It is actually four times.

In order to convince yourself of this fact, take a sheet of paper and place on it two equal sized coins. Then holding the lower one tight in its place, roll the upper coin around it. You will find out to your surprise that by the time the upper coin reaches the bottom of the lower one it will have fully rotated on its axis. And when it has done a complete circle around the lower coin, it will have rotated twice.

Speaking in general, when a body rotates round a circle, it always does one revolution more than one can count. It is precisely this that explains why the earth revolving round the sun succeeds in rotating on its axis not in 365¼ days but in 366¼ days. If one counts its revolutions in respect to the stars and not the sun, you will understand now, why sidereal days are shorter than solar days.

14 0123456789 ....

15 He ate 26 idlis on the fourth day.

Day	No. Eaten
1st day	x
2nd day	$x + 6$
3rd day	$x + 12$
4th day	$x + 18$
5th day	$x + 24$
Total	$5x + 60 = 100;\ x = 8;\ 8 + 18 = 26$

117

16

1	7 2 3 10
2 3	4 5 6
4 5 6	8 9
7 8 9 10	1

17 ½. This problem can be worked by simultaneous equations, but the solution shown below is a more clever, more intuitive approach.

$$\frac{1}{a} + \frac{1}{b} = \frac{a + b}{ab} = \frac{10}{20} = \frac{1}{2}$$

18 The N column is the most restrictive column since it has only four open choices, instead of the five usual choices. These four choices must be made from the set (31, 32, 33 ......43, 44, 45) which contain fifteen elements. Thus when we have made all possible selections of 4 numbers from 15 numbers, we will have reached the total possible number of different Bingo cards.

$$\left(\frac{15}{4}\right) = \frac{15 \times 14 \times 13 \times 12}{4 \times 3 \times 2 \times 1} = 1365$$

19 $888 + 88 + 8 + 8 + 8 = 1000$

Complete answer to Question 19

1) $\dfrac{8 + 8}{8}(8 \times 8 \times 8 - 8) - 8 = 1000$

2) $\dfrac{8888 - 888}{8} = 1000$

3) $\left(\dfrac{88 - 8}{\cdot 8}\right)\left(8 + \dfrac{8 + 8}{8}\right)$ = 1000

4) $\left(8 + \dfrac{8 + 8}{8}\right)\left(8 + \dfrac{8 + 8}{8}\right)$ = 1000

5) $8(8 \times 8 + 8 \times 8) - 8 - 8 - 8$ = 1000

6) $\left[8(8 + 8) - \left(\dfrac{8 + 8 + 8)}{8}\right)\right]8$ = 1000

Using the factorial signs we have:

7) $\dfrac{8!}{8\left(8 - \dfrac{8 + 8 + 8}{8}\right)} - 8$ = 1000

8) $8!\ \dfrac{8 + 8}{8(88 - 8)} - 8$ = 1000

20 There are 47 different triangles

21 I am showing below the possible solutions. The important thing to remember about the problem is that P must be less than four or it would be possible to make change for one rupee:

Asha or Nisha	1P	5P	10P	25P	50P
Asha or Nisha	4	0	4	3	0
Asha or Nisha	4	0	9	1	0

22 S = 112 + 126 + ... 994
S = 14 (8 + 9 + ... 71)

$$S = \frac{14\ (8 + 71)\ (71 - 8 + 1)}{2}$$

$$S = 7(79)\ (64) = 35392$$

23 14 Squares

24

9	9	9

25

13	4¼	10½
6¾	9¼	10¾
8	14¼	5½

26 Let $n = \sqrt{12 + \sqrt{12 + \sqrt{12 + \sqrt{12 + \sqrt{12}}}}}$
the $n^2 = 12 + n$

$n^2 - n - 12 = 0$

$(n - 4)\ (n + 3) = 0$

$n = -3$ or 4 So $n = 4$ Since expression is principal sq. root

27 The hair that falls last is the one that is the youngest today i.e. the one that is only one day old.

Let us now calculate how long it will take before the last hair falls.

121

In the first month a man sheds 3000 hairs out of 150,000 he has on his head.

In the first two months 6000.

And in the first year 3000 x 12 = 36000

Therefore it will take a little over four years for the last hair to fall.

It is in this way that we have determined the average age of human hair.

28 $\left(\dfrac{1}{10} + 1\right)^{10} = \dfrac{11^{10}}{10^{10}} = 2.5937424601$

29 This is a multiplication magic square. The product of each set of three numbers in any column or row is the constant 120.

30 If the son is x years old, then the father is 2x years old. Eighteen years ago they were both eighteen years younger.

The father was 2x - 18 and the son x - 18.

We know that then the father was three times as old as the son:

3(x - 18) = 2x - 18

When we solve this equation, we will find that x = 36.

The son is 36 and the father 72.

31 4 x 21978 = 87912. The number is reversed

32 49

33 If instead of a sari, handbag and shoes if I had bought only two pairs of shoes, I would have had to pay not 140 rupees but as many times less as the shoes are cheaper than the sari and the handbag, i.e. 120 rupees less. Consequently, the two pairs of shoes would have cost 140 – 120 = 20 rupees. Hence one pair costs 10 rupees.

Now we know that the sari and the handbag together cost 140 – 10 = 130 rupees. We also know that the sari is Rs. 90/- more expensive than the handbag. Now let us use the same reasoning again. Had I bought two handbags instead of a sari and a handbag, I would have had to pay not Rs. 130/- but Rs. 90/- less.

Therefore two handbags cost 130 – 90 = 40 rupees. And one handbag costs 20 rupees.

Now we know exactly how much each article cost: Shoes Rs. 10/- Handbag Rs. 20/- Sari Rs. 110/- Rs. 140/- in all.

34 The rule of three means proportion. In the words if three numbers are given when four numbers are in proportion, this is a method of finding one of them.

35
$$8^m = 5/3$$
$$8^m = 32$$
$$(2^3)^m = 2^5$$
$$2^{3m} = 2^5$$
$$3m = 5$$
$$m = 5/3$$

36 $\binom{14}{1} + \binom{14}{2} + \binom{14}{3} + \binom{14}{4} + ... \binom{14}{14} = 2^{14} - 1 = 16383$

37 142857

38 $2^{127} - 1 =$

170 1411 834604692317316873037 15884 105 727

39 $x_n = \left(\dfrac{1}{1} - \dfrac{1}{2}\right) + \left(\dfrac{1}{2} - \dfrac{1}{3}\right) + \left(\dfrac{1}{3} - \dfrac{1}{4}\right)$

$$+ \ldots \left(\dfrac{1}{n} - \dfrac{1}{n+1}\right)$$

$$x_n = 1 + 0 + 0 + 0 + 0 + \ldots \ldots + 0 + 0 + \dfrac{-1}{n+1}$$

$$x_n = 1 - \dfrac{1}{n+1} = \dfrac{n}{n+1}$$

40 The early Romans before Julius Caesar from whom our calendar comes from began the year in March. Therefore December was the tenth month.

However, when New Year was moved to January 1, the names of the months were not shifted, which caused the disparity between the meaning of the names of certain months and their sequence:

Here is an example:

Months	Meaning	Place
September	(Septem–Seven)	9th
October	(Octo–Eight)	10th
November	(Novem–Nine)	11th
December	(Deka–Ten)	12th

41 $\dfrac{5280}{C} = \dfrac{5280}{6\,\pi} = \dfrac{880}{\pi}$

42 15, 21, 28. These are triangular numbers:
1, 3, 6, 10, 15 21 28 .... $\dfrac{n (n + 1)}{2}$

43 This problem would easily lead one to think that the speed we seek is the mean result of 10 and 15 kilometres i.e. 12.5 an hour. But this is wrong.

In fact, if the distance the skier covers is x kilometres, then going at 15 kilometres an hour he will require $\dfrac{x}{15}$ and at 12.5 kilometres $\dfrac{x}{12^{1}/_2}$ or $\dfrac{2x}{25}$

So the equation: $\dfrac{2x}{25} - \dfrac{1}{15} = \dfrac{1}{10} - \dfrac{2x}{25}$

Because each of these is equal to one hour, when we simplify, we obtain: $\dfrac{2}{25} - \dfrac{1}{15} = \dfrac{2}{25}$

Or it can be expressed in arithmetical proportion: $\dfrac{4}{25} = \dfrac{1}{15} + \dfrac{1}{10}$

But this equation is wrong hecause:
$\dfrac{1}{15} + \dfrac{1}{10} = \dfrac{1}{6}$ i.e. $\dfrac{4}{24}$ and not $\dfrac{4}{25}$

But it can be solved orally in the following manner:

If the speed is 15 kilometres an hour and was out for two hours more he would cover an additional 30 kilometres. In one hour, as we already know, he covers 5 kms more. Thus, he would be out for 30:5 = 6 hours. This figure determines the duration of the run at 15 kilometres an hour : 6 – 2 = 4 hours. And now we can easily find the distance covered : 15 x 4 4 = 60 kilometres.

Now, again, without any difficulty we can see how fast he must ski to arrive at the appointed place at 12 noon —— i.e. five hours.

44 $7^3 - 7 \times 48 = 7$

45 2^{29} or 536 870 912
The sum of the coefficients equals the sum of the combinations of twentynine things taken none at a time plus twentynine things taken one at a time.

46 First of all, let us see what happened to the original number. A similar number was written alongside it. It worked out to the same as if we took a number, multiplied it by 100 and then added the original number. For example:

$$872872 = 872000 + 872$$

Here my friend has actually multiplied the original number by 1001. What did he do after that?

He had it divided successfully by 7, 11 and 13 or by 7 x 11 x 13 i.e. by 1001.

So he actually first multiplied the original number by 1001 and then had it divided by 1001. How very simple!

47

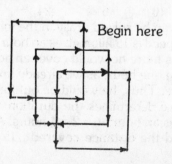

Begin here

126

48 45 Paise, 2 five Paise, 2 ten Paise and 1 twenty five Paise.

49 7, 346, 648, 004, 560, 986, 215, 348, 444, 286, 445, 305, 146, 039, 140, 046, 960, 678, 582, 256, 003.

50 $\frac{1}{7}$. 52 x 7 = 364   364 + 1 = 365 days There are 52 of each day plus 1 extra day. Thus the probability of anyone day of week occurring, in a non-leap Year is one-seventh.

51 Let the change in radius or height be x. Then $(8)^2 (3 + x) = (8 + x)^2 (3)$; x = 16/3

52 When I took half of the string there naturally remained ½. After Deepa took what she wanted there remained ¼. After Amit ⅛ remained. and after Pallavi $\frac{1}{8} \times \frac{3}{5} = \frac{3}{40}$. If 30 cm = $\frac{3}{40}$ then the original length was 30. $\frac{3}{40}$ = 400 cm or 4 metres.

53 $(2^6 - 1) / 2^6 = \frac{63}{64}$

54 $(18 \times 19) + (14 \times 47) = 1000$

55 11

56 Very simple. All you have to do is to find the digit which, added to the two you will get nearest divisible by 9. For example, in 639, I crossed out the 3, and I told him the other two 6 and 9. All he had to do was add them and get 15. The nearest number divisible by 9 is 18. Therefore the missing number is 3.

57 Now we have to see how the numbers are to be placed. Let us assume the following:

The sum of the numbers at the points is 26, while the total of all the numbers of the star is 78. Therefore, the sum of the numbers of the inner hexagon is 78 – 26 = 52.

We shall now proceed on to examine one of the big triangles. The sum of the numbers on each of its sides is 26. If we add up the three sides we get 26 x 3 = 78. But in this case, the numbers at the points will each be counted twice. Since the sum of the numbers of the three inner pairs — i.e. the inner hexagon — must, naturally be 52. Then the doubled sum at points of each triangle is 78 – 52 = 26 or 13 for each triangle.

At this point our search narrows down. We know that neither 12 nor 11 can occupy the circles at the points. So we can try 10 and immediately we come to the conclusion that the other two digits must be 1 and 2.

It is all very simple now. All we have to do is follow up and eventually we shall find the exact arrangement we are looking for, as shown in the figure below:

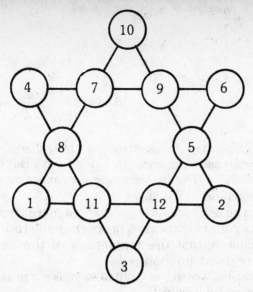

58 1, 3, 9, 27, 81, 243. All powers of three.

59 Let us assume a is 'Diophantus' age
a/6 + a/12 + a/7 + 5 + a/2 + 4
= a; a = 84
Diaphantus lived to be 84 years old

60 24 billion hours later it would be 9 O'clock and 8 hours before that it would be one O'clock.

61 We shall do a simple listing below, which will provide us the solution:

1	2	3	Conditions Met
1	2	3	No

1	3	2	No
2	1	3	No
2	3	1	Yes
3	1	2	Yes
3	2	1	No

Answer is $\dfrac{2}{6}$ or $\dfrac{1}{3}$

62 One may think that the magnifying glass increases our angle to $1^1/2° \times 4 = 6°$. But it is a great mistake. The magnifying glass cannot increase the magnitude of the angle.

Yes, the arc measuring the angle increases, but then its radius increases proportionally too. And the result is that the magnitude of the central angle remains unchanged.

It may be worth your while to make a practical experiment with this.

63 One of the fathers is the son of the other father. The problem posed would seem as if there are altogether four persons concerned. But that is not so. The three persons are grandfather, father and son. The grandfather gave his son Rs. 150/- and the latter passed on Rs. 100/- of them to the grandson (i.e. his son). Thus increasing his own money by Rs. 50/-.

64

Sin 30°	$\dfrac{1}{2}$	Sin 60°	$\dfrac{\sqrt{3}}{2}$
Cos 30°	$\dfrac{\sqrt{3}}{2}$	Cos 60°	$\dfrac{1}{2}$
Tan 30°	$\dfrac{1}{\sqrt{3}}$	Tan 60°	$\sqrt{3}$
Cotn 30°	3	Cot 60°	$\dfrac{1}{\sqrt{3}}$

| Sec 30° | $\dfrac{2}{\sqrt{3}}$ | Sec 60° | 2 |
| Csc 30° | 2 | Csc 60° | $\dfrac{2}{\sqrt{3}}$ |

65 You will be stunned at the answer. The pole would be 1000 kilometres high. Let us try to calculate it mentally.

A cubic metre equals: 1000 cubic millimetre × 1000 × 1000.

One thousand millimetre cubes placed one atop another will make a pole 1 metre in height. And since we have 1000 × 1000 times more cubes, we shall have a pole that is 1000 kilometres long.

66 No one knows!

67 The total of all the numbers on a clock face is 78. And so that total of each of the six parts should be 78 : 6 = 13.

This helps to find the solution as shown in the figure above.

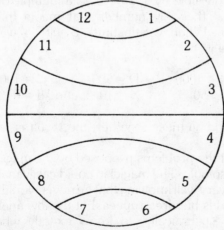

68 An essential fact we must know before we start solving the problem, we must know how many legs the spider and the beetle have. From the study of natural science, we know that spiders have 8 legs and beetles 6.

Let us now assume that there were only beetles in the box — 8 of them. Then there should be 48 legs, or 6 less than mentioned in the problem.

Now if we substitute one spider for one of the beetles, the number of legs will increase by 2, because the spider has 8 legs and not 6.

It is now clear that if we substitute three spiders for three beetles we shall bring the number of legs in the box to the required 54. In that case, instead of 8 beetles we shall have 5. The rest will be spiders.

Now we can conclude that the boy collected 5 beetles and 3 spiders: 5 beetles have 30 legs and 3 spiders have 24 legs. In all the boy collected 54 legs.

69 If S434S0 is to be divisible by 36, then it is also divisible by 4 and 9. To be divisible by 4 S must be an even number.

To be divisible by 9, 25 + 11 is a multiple of 9. The digit '8' is the only number that meets these two conditions. When we substitute 'S' with '8' we get the Ans: 843480.

70 M = 1000   D = 500   C = 100
L = 50   X = 10   and VI = 6

If we add all these together, the result is 1666.

71 All the problems proposed by the magician are insoluble. The magician could easily make such an offer, very well knowing that he never would have to part with his hundred rupees. Let us now analyse the problem algebraically, to know exactly where the magician had his safety valve:

132

To pay 5 rupees : Let us assume that it is necessary for us to have 'a' number of 50P coins, 'b' number of 20P coins and 'c' number of 5P coins. Then we will have the equation:

$50a + 20b + 5c = 500 P = 5$ rupees.

Simplifying this we get : $10a + 4b + c = 100$

However, according to the problem, the total number of coins is 20, and therefore we have the other equation: $a + b + c = 20$

When we subtract · this equation from the first we get: $9a + 3b = 80$

Dividing this by 3 we obtain: $3a + b = 26\,^2/_3$. But 3a i.e. the number of 50 P coins multiplied by 3 is, of course, an integer like b, the number of 20 P coins. And the sum of these two numbers cannot be a fractional number. Therefore the problem is insoluble. In the same way the 'reduced' payment problem are also similarly insoluble. In the case of Rs. 3/- we get the following equation: $3a \times b = 13^1/_2$

And in the case of Rs. 2/- we get the equation: $3a + b = 6^2/3$

Both, as we can see, are fractional numbers. Therefore the magician risked nothing in making such a generous offer. But it would have been another thing altogether had he asked for Rs. 4/- instead of Rs. 5/-, Rs. 3/- or Rs. 2/-. Then we could have found seven different solutions to the problem.

72 **Cycloid.** Cycloid is the simplest member of the class of curves known as roulettes and it was not known before the 15 Century. And it was seriously studied until the 17th Century.

Many great mathematicians like Descartes, Pascal, Lisbuitz, the Bermoullis and others have investigated the properties of the Cycloid that it was sometimes named the 'Helen on Geometers'.

73

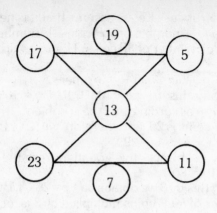

74

370, 371, 407.

75

a) =   9 = 3²
b) = 16 = 4²
c) = 25 = 5²
d) = 36 = 6²
e) = 49 = 7²
f) = 64 = 8²
g) = 81 = 9²
h) = $\dfrac{(291 + 1)^2}{2}$ = 21316
i) = $(\dfrac{R + 1}{2})^2$

76

a) In a given circle O, draw a diameter $\overline{AB}$
b) Construct $\overline{CD}$ as perpendicular bisector of $\overline{AB}$

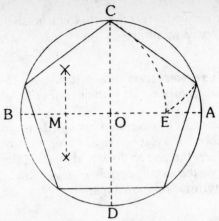

c) Bisect OB, label its centre M.
d) Using M as a centre and CM as a radius, draw an arc intersecting AO at E.
e) CE is the required length of one side of the inscribed pentagon.

77 First of all let us find out how the typists should divide the job to finish it at the same time.

The more experienced typist, that is Mr. Das Gupta, can work 1½ times faster than the other. Therefore it is clear that his share of work should be 1½ times greater. Then Mr Das Gupta as well as the new lady typist will both finish the work simultaneously.

Hence Mr Das Gupta should take ³/₅ of the work and the lady typist ²/₅.

This solves the problem, but there still remains for us to find how long it takes Mr. Das Gupta to do his share i.e. ³/₅ of the work.

We know that he can do the whole job in two hours. Therefore ³/₅ of job will be done in ³/₅ × 2 = 1¹/₅ hours.

So the other typist also must finish her share of work within the same time.

Therefore the fastest time they can finish the work is 1 hour and 12 minutes.

78 There were two girls and a boy, their father and mother, and their father's father and mother.

As it would be too much for words to go into the explanations of relationships here, the most satisfactory thing for you to do would be to sit down, write out a list of the seven people involved, and check off the twentythree relationships.

79

$$3^3 + 4^3 + 5^3 = 27 + 64 + 125 = 216 = 6^3$$
$$1^3 + 6^3 + 8^3 = 1 + 216 + 512 = 729 = 9^3$$
$$25^3 + 38^3 + 87^3 = 15625 + 54872 + 658503 = 729000 = 90^3$$

80 While solving this problem, we must bear in mind the rule governing the divisibility of a number by 11.

A number is divisible by 11 if the difference of the sums between the sums of the odd digits and the even digits, counting from the right, is divisible 11 or equal to 0.

Let us, for example, try the number 49836781.
The sum of the even digits : $9 + 3 + 7 + 1 = 20$
The sum of the odd digits : $4 + 5 + 6 + 8 = 23$

81 The crescent may be divided in six parts as shown in the diagram. The six parts are numbered for the sake of convenience.

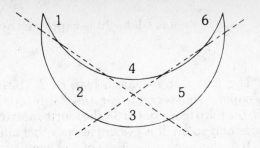

82 M D C C L X X X I X

83 The model is 8000000 times lighter than the real Eiffel Tower. Both are made of the same metal, and so the volume of the model should be 8000000 times less than that of the real tower.

We know that the volumes of similar figures are to one another as the cubes of their altitudes.

Therefore, the model must be 200 times smaller than the original because 200 x 200 x 200 = 8,000000

The altitude of the real tower is 300 metres; and so the height of the model should be 300 : 200 = 1½ metres.

Then the model will be about the height of a man.

84 1408 hours is actually 8 minutes past 2 P.M. This is the system of twenty-four-hour clock. Writing the hours and minutes this way is a sensible means of avoiding any confusion between A.M. and P.M.

This system which is commonly used in the railway time tables in continent of Europe leave no possible doubt about the time of the day or night when a train is due to leave a station. Midnight is expressed as 0000 hours.

85 The first tear results in two, or 2^1, pieces of paper. The second tear results in four or 2^2 pieces, the third tear eight or 2^3, the fourth in sixteen or 2^4 pieces and so on. It is evident at once that after the fiftieth tear the stack will consist of 2^{50} sheets of paper which equals — 11258 9990 6842 624

Now, we know that there are a thousand sheets to the inch. Therefore the stack will be about 1125899906842 inches high.

To get the height of the stack in feet we have to divide this number by 12 and to get it in miles we have to divide the resulting number by 5280. The final result will be well over 17,000,000 miles.

86 Harmonic Progression. This is sometimes abbreviated to H.P. (Don't confuse it as Horse Power or the sauce).

87 $360°$

88 Fibonacci series. In this series the sum of the 2nd and 3rd terms equals the 4th term, the sum of the 3rd and 4th term equals the 5th term, the sum of the 4th and 5th term equals the 5th term and so on all the way through the series.

This series is named after Fibonacci, who was born in 1175.

Fibonacci thought that his series of numbers

solved many problems connected with plant growth and it was found to be true that the positions and numbers of the leaves on the stems of certain plants are connected by the series.

89 6. 7. 8.,   7. 8. 9.   8. 9. 10

90 One would quickly come out with the answer, 1 kilogramme, that is four times less. But this is absolutely wrong.

The smaller brick is not only four times shorter than the real one, but it is also four times narrower and four times lower and therefore its volume and weight are 4 x 4 x 4 = 64 times.

The correct answer would be : 4000 : 64 = 62.5 Grammes.

91 Now let's see how this could have been done with the least possible number of moves.

To start with let us assume that we had only two coins 25 P and 5 P, and not five. How many moves would we require then ?

We would exactly require three moves. The 25 P coin would go into the middle saucer, the 5 P coin into the third and then the 25 P comes over it.

Now let us add one more coin to this — three instead of two, 25 P, 5 P and 10 P. We shall now see how many moves we need to transpose the pile.

First we move the two smaller coins in the middle saucer, and to do that as we already know we need three moves. Then we move the 10 P coin to the third saucer. That is one more move. Then we move the two coins from the second saucer, to the third and that makes it another three moves. Therefore, we have to do altogether 7 moves.

For four coins we need 15 moves and for 5 coins we will need 31 moves.

An interesting pattern can be noted from the above calculations.

The numbers we obtained are :

Coins	Moves	Pattern	
2	3	2 × 2 – 1	= $2^2 - 1$
3	7	2 × 2 × 2 – 1	= $2^3 - 1$
4	15	2 × 2 × 2 × 2 – 1	= $2^4 - 1$
5	31	2 × 2 × 2 × 2 – 1	= $2^5 - 1$

So the easiest way to find out the number of moves is to multiply 2 by itself as many times as there are coins to be transposed and then subtract 1.

For instance if there are eight coins the operation would be as follows :

2 × 2 × 2 × 2 × 2 × 2 × 2 × 2 – 1 or $2^8 - 1$

And ten coins :

2 × 2 × 2 × 2 × 2 × 2 × 2 × 2 × 2 × 2 – 1 = $2^{10} - 1$

92 Approximately 24 feet.

$8 + 4 + 4 + 2 + 2 + 1 + 1 + \frac{1}{2} + \frac{1}{2} + \frac{1}{4} + \frac{1}{4} + \frac{1}{8} \ldots\ldots =$

$8 + 2 (4 + 2 + 1 + \frac{1}{2} + \frac{1}{4} + \frac{1}{8} + \ldots\ldots\ldots) \quad =$

$8 + 2 (4 + 2) + 2 (2) = 24$

$8 + 12 + 2(2) (1 + \frac{1}{2} + \frac{1}{4} + \frac{1}{8} \ldots\ldots) =$

$S_n = 1 + (\frac{1}{2})^1 + (\frac{1}{2})^2 + \ldots\ldots + (\frac{1}{2})^{n-1}$

$\frac{1}{2} S_n = (\frac{1}{2}) + (\frac{1}{2})^2 + (\frac{1}{2})^3 \ldots\ldots + (\frac{1}{2})^{n-1} + (\frac{1}{2})^n$

Subtracting the second line from the first, we have

$S_n (1\frac{1}{2}) = 1 - (\frac{1}{2})^n$

And therefore :

$S_n = (1-\frac{1}{2})^n = 2 - (\frac{1}{2})^{n-1}$

Since n increases indefinitely, $\frac{1}{2}^{n-1}$ approaches zero and S_n approaches 2 as a limit.

$$\frac{1 - (\frac{1}{2})n}{S_n = \frac{1}{2}} \qquad = 2 - (\frac{1}{2})^{n-1}$$

93 44, 36 — The odd terms increase by 9 each time, and the even terms increase by 7 each time.

94 To solve this problem, we shall have to start from the end.

We have been told that after all the transpositions, the number of matches in each heap is the same. Let us proceed from this fact.

Since the total number of matches has not changed in the process, and the total number being 48, it follows that there were 16 matches in each heap.

And so, in the end we have: First Heap: 16, Second Heap: 16, Third Heap: 16

Immediately before this we have added to the first heap as many matches as there were in it, i.e. we had doubled the number. So, before the final transposition, there are only 8 matches in the first heap.

Now, in the third heap, from which we took these 8 matches, there were: 16 + 8 = 24 matches.

We now have the numbers as follows: First Heap: 8, Second Heap: 16, Third Heap: 24.

We know that we took from the second heap as many matches as there were in the third heap, which means 24 was double the original number. From this we know how many matches we had in each heap after the first transposition:

First Heap: 8, Second Heap: 16 + 12 = 28, Third Heap: 12.

Now we can draw the final conclusion that before the first transposition the number of matches in each heap was:

First Heap: 22, Second Heap: 14, Third Heap: 12.

95 Here is the completed magic square:

67	1	43
13	37	61
31	73	7

To find the solution, we must, first of all find the number in the central cell which in this case is ½ (43 + 31) or 37.

When this diagonal is complete, we know total for each diagonal, row and column — which in this example is 111.

In this way you build up the entire magic square cell by all.

96 588 = 7 x 84;   4200 = 50 x 84; Yes

97 There are also other solutions.

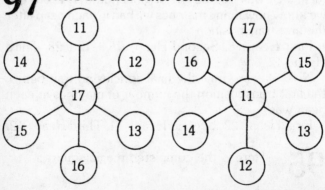

98 Each term in this series is a factorial, in other words, the product of all the numbers from 1 to the particular term considered. The first five terms of the series are, therefore 1, 2, 6, 24, 120 and the sum of these numbers is 153.

99 No. Knitting needles conform to the Standard Wire Guage (S. W. G.) sizes, and the larger the S. W. G. number, the smaller is the diameter of the wire.

100 The thirtieth set would consist of: 2^{30} = 1073 74 1824 letters

The first set consists of 2 or 2^1 letters.
The second set consists of 4 or 2^2 letters.
The third set consists of 8 or 2^3 letters.
And therefore the 30th set would consist of 2^{30} letters.

101 Here are four solutions. But with patience and pencil work you can find more:

765	859	364	849
324	743	725	357
----	----	----	----
1089	1602	1089	1206

102 (150 – 1) = 149, since all but one lose one game.

103 78, 116 The odd terms are in the decimal system and differ by 10. And each even term is the preceding odd term expressed in the octonary system. 78 – 8 = 9, remainder 6:9 : 8 = 1, remainder 1.

104 (7/16) x 9 + 10½ seconds

143

105 6 men pack 6 boxes in 6 minutes
6 men pack 1 box in 1 minute
6 men pack 60 boxes in 60 minutes

106

Primes	Composites
163	$161 = 7 \times 23$
167	$169 = 13^2$
293	$187 = 11 \times 17$
367	$289 = 17^2$

107 First the two sons rowed across the river and one stayed behind while the other returned in the boat to his father. The son remained behind while the father crossed the river. Then the other son brought back the boat and the two brothers rowed over together.

108 9^{9^9}

9^9 means the product of 9 nines.

$9 \times 9 \times 9 \times 9 \times 9 \times 9 \times 9 \times 9 \times 9 = 387420489$

9^{9^9} would mean $9^{387420489}$ or the product of 387420489 nines.

This claculation would require more than three hundred and eightyseven million multiplications and at the rate of one digit per second, it would require nearly twelve years to write the number.

109 It is not a prime number. 1757051 x 1291 x 1361

144

110 The value of Pi to seven places of decimals are contained in this mnemonic. The number of letters in each word corresponds to the successive integers in the decimal expansion of Pi.

111 One minute and thirtynine seconds, because when the ninetyninth cut is made, the remaining foot does not have to be cut.

112 Lalitha got 3 and Vasantha 5. I ate my share of the gooseberries which was 61/3. Therefore there were 2/3 of the gooseberries left in the bowl.

Lalitha took her 1/3 of these or 1/3 of 2/3 = 2/9 of them.

So when Vasantha arrived already 1/3 + 2/9 = 5/9 of the original gooseberries had been eaten. Therefore only 4/9 of the original number of the gooseberries remained from which Vasantha proceeded to eat her share.

Therefore Vasantha ate 1/3 of 4/9 and there remained 2/3 of 4/9 = 8/27.

But in the evening we saw that eight gooseberries remained in the bowl.

Therefore 8/27 of the original number = 8.

So there were 27 gooseberries in the bowl when I first took my share of 9.

I was the only one to have had my fair share of the gooseberries.

Lalitha took what she thought was her share, from the remaining 18 gooseberries namely 6. And from the remaining 12 Vasantha had taken 4 gooseberries thinking that to be her share.

Now after Lalitha got her 3 and Vasantha her 5 gooseberries, we all had eaten an even share of 9 gooseberries each.

113 The googol is: 10,000, 000, 000, 000, 000, 000, 000, 000, 000, 000, 000, 000, 000, 000, 000, 000, 000, 000, 000, 000, 000, 000, 000, 000, 000, 000, 000, 000, 000, 000, 000, 000.

114 22½°   The hour hand moves same fraction of the distance between two and three (30°) as the minute hand has moved of a complete rotation
($^1/_4$)

$$30 - \frac{1}{4}(30) = 30 - 7\frac{1}{2} = 22\frac{1}{2}$$

115 If there were x children at the party then the two ways of distributing the candy can be represented by these two expressions:

$3(x - 1) + 2$ and $2x + 8$

$\therefore 3x - 3 + 2 = 2x + 8$

or $x = 9$

The number of candy for distribution = $2 \times 9 + 8 = 26$

116 The train leaving Mysore travels faster, and naturally they meet and cross one another nearer to Bangalore.

The meeting place is 40/90 of 60 or 26-2/3 miles from Bangalore and 50/90 of 60 or 33-1/3 miles from Mysore, and this happens at 10-40 A. M.

117 This is a typical example of a problem with geometrical basis, disguised by extraneous details. It is impossible to solve this problem without geometry.

The question is why does the front axle wear out faster than the rear. We know from Geometry that the cricle with a smaller circumference has to make more revolutions than the bigger circle to cover the same distance. And, naturally, the wheel turns more often, and quicker the front axle wears out.

118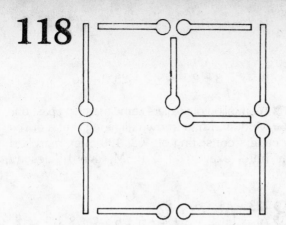

119 1973, 1979, 1987, 1993, 1997, 1999

120 Circumferences are to one another as their diameters. If the circumference of one pumpkin in 60 centimetres and of the other 50 centimetres, then the ratio between their diameters is:

60 : 50 = 6/5 and the ratio between their sizes is: $(6/5)^3$ = 216/125 = 1.73

The bigger pumpkin, if it were priced according to its size or weight should cost 1.73 times or 73 per cent more than the small one. Yet the vendor has priced it only 50 per cent more. Therefore, it is clear, that the bigger pumpkin is a better bargain.

121 8, 12, 5, 20
A + B + C + D = 45
A + 2 = B – 2 = 2C = D/2
A = B – 4 ; C = $\frac{B – 2}{2}$; D = 2(B – 2)

B – 4 + B – 2 + 2(B – 2) = 45
2

B = 12
A = 8
C = 5
D = 20
Thus: 12 – 2 = 8 + 2 = 5 x 2 = 20/2 = 10

122 A battalion of soldiers came marching past our window. I had known all along that a corps of army cadets consisting of over 100 men, marched past our hotel exactly at 2 P. M. every Tuesday afternoon.

123 123 – 45 – 67 + 89
Also 1 + 2 + 3 + 4 + 5 + 6 + 7 + 8 x 9

124 1152 cubic centimetres.
Let us assume v is the volume of the box, and x be the side of the squares cut out.

Then $v = (32 - 2x)(20 - 2x)x$

or $v = 640x - 104x^2 + 4x^3$

$$\therefore \frac{dv}{dx} = 640 - 208x + 12x^2$$

For a maximum volume $\frac{dv}{dx} = 0$

or $3x^2 - 52x + 160 = 0$
or $(3x - 40)(x - 4) = 0$
or $x = 4$ or $x = \frac{40}{3}$

The real volume of x can only be 4. Therefore the maximum volume of the box is 24 x 12 x 4 = 1152 cubic centimetres.

125 Yes. Vasantha did. The person listening to the radio hears the given note first.

126

a – 5   b – 13   c – 27   d – 48

127

12 inches. The diagonal of the end is 5. Therefore the space diagonal will be the hypotenuse of a right angle, one of whose legs is 5, the other an integer.

Three numbers, known as the Pythagorean Triples, can be represented by:

m_1 ½ $(m^2 - 1)$ and ½$(m^2 + 1)$ because

$m_2 + (½(m^2 - 1))^2 = (½ (m^2 + 1))^2$

$5^2 + 12^2 = 13^2$. The other dimension is 12 inches. Therefore the space diagonal is 13 inches.

128

Here again there is an example of a problem that does not seem mathematical at all at the first glance but a closer look will reveal that this is a problem that cannot be solved without geometry.

We all know that things usually cool down from the surface. So, a child standing out in the street, in the cold, feels the cold more than a similarly dressed adult, though the amount of heat in each cubic centimetre of the body is almost the same in the case of both.

A child has a greater cooling surface per one cubic centimetre of the body than an adult.

This also explains why a person's fingers and nose suffer more from cold and get frost bitten oftener than any other parts of the body whose surface is not so great when compared to their volume.

This same theory explains why splint wood catches fire faster than the log from which it has been chopped off. Heat spreads from the surface to the whole volume of a body and therefore the heat sets splint wood on fire faster than the log.

129

Suppose x is the diagonal of the floor. Then $x^2 = 24^2 + 48^2$, $x = 24\sqrt{5}$

And if h is the height of the room, then
$h^2 + (24\sqrt{5})^2 = 56^2$ and h = 16.
Thus the height of the room is 16 ft.

130

Time required for the first
sixty miles   : 120 minutes
Time required for the second sixty miles
            : 72 minutes
Total time required   : 192 minutes

I travelled 120 miles in 192 minutes. Therefore the average speed in miles per hour was: $\dfrac{60 \times 120}{192} = 37\frac{1}{2}$

131

This is the only known number that is a sum of two cubes in two different ways.
Example: $10^3 + 9^3 = 1729$, $12^3 + 1^3 = 1729$

This is popularly known as Ramanujam's number. There is an interesting story about it. The story goes this way. When Ramanujam was sick in the hospital, Prof. Hardy, his tutor paid him a visit. Prof. Hardy told Ramanujam that he rode a taxicab to the hospital, with a very unlucky number.

When Ramanujam enquired what the number was, Prof. Hardy replied: 1729.

Ramanujam's face lit up with a smile and he said that it was not an unlucky number at all, but a very interesting number, the only number that can be represented as the sum of two cubes in two different ways!

132
19 days.

133
Pi to 30 decimal places.

134

We must, first of all separate the sum into two parts, x and y.

$$X = \frac{1}{7} + \frac{1}{7^3} + \frac{1}{7^5} + \ldots\ldots \frac{1}{7^{2n-1}}$$

$$Y = \frac{2}{7^2} + \frac{2}{7^4} + \frac{2}{7^6} \ldots\ldots \frac{2}{7^{2n}}$$

$$X = \frac{\dfrac{1}{7}}{1 - 7^2} = \frac{7}{48}$$

$$Y = \frac{\dfrac{2}{7^2}}{1 - \dfrac{1}{7^2}} = \frac{2}{48}$$

$$\frac{7}{48} + \frac{2}{48} = \frac{9}{48} = \frac{3}{16}$$

135

Supposing the change in radius or height be x.

Then $(8)^2 (3 + x) = (8 + x)^2 (3)$

$$x = \frac{16}{3}$$

136

1048576 — 400 years ago, that is 20 generations back, Ram — for that matter each one of us had 2^{20} or 1048576 ancestors.

137

About 109 years

138

No. 1000009 = 293 x 3413

151

139

$$\left(\frac{26}{6}\right) \div \left(\frac{52}{(6)}\right) = \frac{253}{22372}$$

140

$$17x = 17 + x$$
$$17x - x = 17$$
$$16x = 17$$
$$x = \frac{17}{16}$$

141

She solved 95 problems correctly
Let us assume W = Wrong and R = Right

$$R - 2W = 85$$
$$\underline{R + W = 100}$$

$$-3W = -15$$
$$W = 5$$
$$W = 5 R = 95$$

142

There are three possible outcomes:
G – B, B – G or G – G. Since only one of these three is girls the probability is $1/3$

143

40 boys.
Let G represent the number of girls in the original group and B the number of boys in the original group. Then we have:

$$\frac{G}{B-15} = \frac{2}{1} \quad \text{and} \quad \frac{G-45}{B-15} = \frac{1}{5}$$

then G = 2(B – 15)
$$5(G - 45) = (B - 15)$$

152

Solving the simultaneous equations above we get:
B = 40 and G = 50

144 1184 – 6368, 5020 – 2924,
2620 – 5564, 6232 – 1210

145 P = 1. She is certain to get a pair.

146 No. 222221 = 619 x 359

147 The area of the edge of the paper which is a rectangle equals the area of the end of the roll. If the radius of the roll is R, then $R^2 = W1$ or $1 = R^2/W$

148 25, 11, 7—First of all we must consider even-odd possibilities for A + B + C = 43

A, B and C must all be odd or two of the three numbers must be even and the other odd. Let us, to start with, investigate the case where all three are odd.

By using a table of cubes, we can see that the unit digit of A, B and C must be odd — 1, 3, 5, 7, or 9. Also we can see the following pattern:

Unit Digit A	Unit Digit B	Unit Digit C	Unit Digit of A+B+C
1	1	1	3*
3	3	3	9
5	5	5	5
7	7	7	1
9	9	9	7
5	7	9	1
3	7	9	9
3	5	9	7
3	5	7	5

1	7	9	7
1	5	9	5
1	5	7	3 *
1	3	9	3 *
1	3	7	1
1	3	5	9

Now it is clear that we only need to consider the three cases where 3 appears in the last column i.e. (1, 1, 1), (1, 5, 7) and (1, 3 9).

Unit Digit A	Unit Digit B	Unit Digit C	Unit Digit of $A^3+B^3+C^3$
1	1	1	3
1	5	7	9 x
1	3	9	7

Now we need consider only one or two digit numbers with unit digits 1, 5 and 7. And the possible value for the ten's digits of A, B and C are 0, 0, 3 or 0, 1, 2.

$31^3 > 17299$ therefore 35^3 and 37^3 are too large.

$27^3 > 17299$

$25^3 = 15625$

$11^3 = 1331$

$07^3 = 343$ Sum total = 17299

Now I leave it to the reader the investigation of the case where two of A, B, C are even and the other odd.

149

$$L. W = 2(L + W) \qquad W - 2 = 1 \text{ or } W-2 = 2$$

$$L = \frac{2W}{W - 2} \qquad W = 3 \text{ or } W = 4$$

Thus a 4 x 4 rectangle or a 3 x 6 rectangle meets the conditions.

150^{Rs 563/31}

151 Thus goes the Benediktov story: 'The problem was a tricky one and the three daughters discussed it on 'their way to the market, with the second and third appealing to the eldest for advice. The latter thought for a while and then said:

'Look, sisters, we'll sell our eggs even at a time and not ten as we always do. We'll fix a price for seven eggs and stick to it, as mother has told us to. Mind you, don't reduce the price however much people may bargain! We'll ask three kopeks for the first seven eggs, all right?'

'That's pretty cheap!' the second sister interjected.

'Never mind,' the eldest retorted, 'we'll raise the price for the eggs that remain after that. I have made sure that there won't be any other egg vendors at the market. So there'll be no one to force our prices down. And when there's a demand for eggs and not many of them are left, the price goes up, that's only natural. And that's exactly where we'll make up.'

'And how much shall we ask for the remaining eggs?' the youngest sister asked.

'Nine kopeks an egg. And believe me, people who need eggs will pay the price.'

'That's pretty stiff,' the second sister remarked. 'So what? The first seven-egg batches will be cheap. The expensive eggs will make up for the loss.'

'The sisters agreed.

'At the market each chose a place. The cheap price brought on an avalanche of buyers and the youngest, who had 50 eggs, soon sold all her eggs but one. At three kopeks per seven eggs she made 21 kopeks. The second sister, who had 30 eggs, made 12 kopeks by selling four people seven eggs each, and had two eggs left in the basket. The eldest made 3 kopeks from the sale of seven eggs and was left with three eggs.

'Suddenly a cook appeared with instructions to buy ten eggs. Her mistress's sons had come home on leave and they loved omlette. The cook rushed about the market, but the only vendors were the three sisters and then they had only six eggs — the youngest had one, the second two and the eldest three.

'It is only natural that the cook rushed to the one who had three — that is, to the eldest sister who had sold her batch of seven eggs for 3 kopeks.

'How much d'you want for your eggs?' she asked.

'Nine kopeks an egg,' was the reply.

'What! You're crazy!'

'Take them or leave them. These are my last and I won't take a kopek less.'

'The cook ran to the second sister, the one who had two eggs left in her basket.

'How much?' she yelled.

'Nine kopeks an egg. That's the price and these are my last eggs.'

'And how much do you want for your egg?' the cook turned to the youngest sister.

'Nine kopeks.'

'Well, there was nothing the cook could do, so she bought the eggs at this exorbitant price.

'All right,' she burst out, 'I'll take the lot.'

'She paid 27 kopeks to the eldest sister for her three eggs and with the three kopeks the latter had from the earlier sale this brought her total receipts to 30 kopeks. The second sister got 18 kopeks and with the 12 kopeks she had received earlier that also made 30 kopeks. The youngest got 9 kopeks for the remaining egg and that, added to the 21 kopeks she had made on the sale of 49 eggs, brought the total also to 30 kopeks.

'The three sisters then returned home, gave the

money to their mother and told her how, sticking to the price they had agreed upon, they had succeeded in selling ten eggs for the same price as 50.

'Their mother was very pleased that her instructions had been carried out and that her eldest daughter had proved so clever. But she was even happier that her daughters had brought her exactly what she had told them to bring — 90 kopeks.'

152 0 (Zero)

153

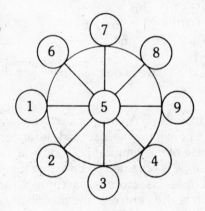

154 CLXVI = 166

155 Circumscribed. The meaning of to circumscribe, to describe a figure round another so as to touch it at points without cutting it.

This is exactly what takes place with a circumscribed circle.

To find the centre of such a circle, we have to bisect

the sides of a triangle and erect perpendiculars, which are concurrent at the circumcentre.

The radius R of the circumscribed circle of the triangle ABC is given by:

$$R = \frac{a}{2 \operatorname{Sin} A} = \frac{b}{2 \operatorname{Sin} B} = \frac{c}{2 \operatorname{Sin} C}$$

156
(1) $x + 9$
(2) $(x + 9)^2 = x^2 + 18x + 81$
(3) $x^2 + 18x + 81 - x^2 = 18x + 81$
(4) $18x + 81 - 61 = 18x + 20$
(5) $2(18x + 20) = 36x + 40$
(6) $(36x + 40) + 24 = 36x + 64$
(7) $36x + 64 - 36x = 64$
(8) $\sqrt{64} + 8$

The answer will always be the same since the variable term drops out.

157 Inscribed. A circle is said to be inscribed in a polygon when each side is tangential to the circle. In case of the simplest polygon — a triangle, the inscribed circle is obtained by bisecting the angles of a triangle. These bisectors pass through a common point which is the centre of the inscribed circle.

158 Scientists have worked it out — though only approximately: The Sun has existed — 10, 000, 000, 000, 000 years.

159 $4 \times 25 + 4 = 100 + 4 = 104$ poles

160 8184—We start out with 2 couples, four people or 2^2 people who increase their progeny as follows:

$2^3 + 2^4 + 2^5 + 2^6 + 2^7 + 2^8 + 2^9 + 2^{10} + 2^{11} + 2^{12} = 8184$

161 Their burdens were 7 and 5.

162 Scientists have worked it out — though approximately: The earth has existed ....2000000000 years.

163 Orthogonal: Orthogonal means 'right–angled'. In other words pertaining to or depending upon the use of right angles. If any curves cut at right angles, they are said to intersect orthogonally.

Such curves are of interest in many branches of applied mathematics. A point of interest about two circles cutting orthogonally is that the square of the distance between the centres is equal to the sum of the squares of their radii.

164 The problem may seem tricky, but it is actually very simple.

Let the diameter of lump sugar be 100 times of powdered sugar. And let us assume that the diameter of the sugar particles and the cup which they fill increase 100 times. Then the capacity of the cup will increase $100 \times 100 \times 100 = 1000000$ times proportionally.

Next, let us measure out an ordinary cup of such enlarged powdered sugar i.e. one millionth part of the contents of our giant cup. It will, of course, weigh exactly the same as an ordinary glass of ordinary powdered sugar.

Then the question arises, what does our enlarged powdered sugar represent? Just a lump of sugar.

Lump sugar is geometrically similar to powdered sugar and it makes no difference if we enlarge a sugar particle 60 times instead of 100. A cup of lump sugar weighs the same as a cup of powdered sugar.

165 71 and 17, 82 and 28 and 93 and 39.

Suppose X be the digit in the unit's place and Y be the digit in the ten's place of the larger number.

Then the larger number is $(10Y + X)$.

And the smaller number is $(10X + Y)$.

And the difference between them is $(10Y + X) - (10X + Y) = 54$.

or $Y - X = 6$

We know that Y cannot be greater than 9 and X cannot be less than 1 and $Y - X$ is exactly 6.

Considering these conditions there are only three possibilities for Y and X namely the pairs 9 and 3, 8 and 2, and 7 and 1.

166 The man who is twice taller outweighs the other not two, but eight times.

167 The only way is to arrange the children in the form of a hexagon, as shown in the diagram.

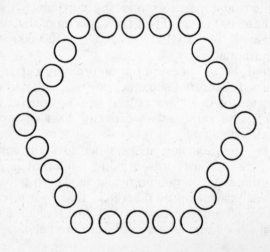

168

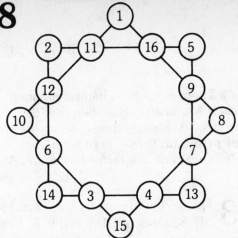

169 3922 ÷ 4 = 980 with remainder 2.
The switch is off.

170 573 Metres—Let a small angular movement
take place during a small displacement
ds. Then if R is the radius of the circle in
which it moves:

$$\frac{1}{R} = \frac{d\theta}{ds}$$

$$\therefore ds = R\, d\theta$$

$$\therefore S = R \int \pi/6\, d\theta$$
$$= R\ [\ \theta\ ]°\ \pi/6$$

$$\therefore 2.150 = R.\ \pi/6, 0$$

$$\therefore R = 573\ \text{metres}.$$

171 −342, 1189—The only way to obtain the law in
this case is by the system of trials.

$$T_n = 5T_{n-2} - 2T_{n-1}$$

Hence $T_8 = (5X - 28) - (2 \times 101) = -342$

172
There is no such natural number.
If A is a natural number, then $2A^2$ cannot be a square since A^2 can be represented as the product of **pairs of prime factors**. There is no 'extra' factor of two to 'pair up with' the factor of two in $2A^2$.

173
The next two numbers are : 13 and 31; 102, 201. Squares are 169 and 961; 10404 and 40401.

174 $11/5$

Since $\left(x - \dfrac{8}{5} \right) \left(x + \dfrac{7}{3} \right) = 0$ $x^2 + \dfrac{11}{5} x - \dfrac{56}{15}$

175 72^2 or 5784

176
There is only one way of finding a solution to this problem: Numbers which leave a remainder of 1, when divided by 2: 3, 5, 7, 9, 11, 13, 15, 17, 19, 21, 23, 25, 27, 29, 31, 33, 35.

Numbers which leave a remainder of 1, when divided by 3: 4, 7, 10, 13, 16, 19, 22, 25, 28, 31, 34, 37.....

Numbers which leave a remainder of 1, when divided by 4: 5, 9, 13, 17, 21, 25, 29, 33, 37.

Numbers which leave no remainder when divided by 5: 5, 10, 15, 20, 25, 30, 35.

The only number fulfilling the four conditions is 25.

177 8 Litres — We must remember that a volume has three dimensions. And when each is doubled according to the question, the new volume is 2 x 2 x 2 times the original volume.

178 60 — Let x equal the number of guests. The number of dishes shared:

$$\frac{x}{2} + \frac{x}{3} + \frac{x}{4} = 65$$

$$\therefore \quad 6x + 4x + 3x = 65 \times 12$$

$$\therefore \quad 13x = 65 \times 12$$

$$\therefore \quad x = \frac{65 \times 12}{13} = 60$$

179 20 Triangles

180 4 daughters and 3 sons. Consider d = number of daughters, and s = number of sons[.] then

d – 1 = s

2(s – 1) = d

Solving d and s,

d = 4,   s = 3

181

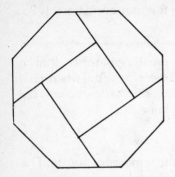 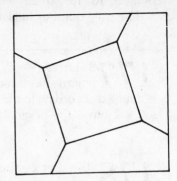

182 **Nine:** I won three games and thus I win 3 ps. Asha has to win back these three pennies which takes another three games. And finally Asha wins three more games to win the total sum of three more ps.

183 Finding a Square with the same Area as a given Circle is a problem which confronted even the Greek Mathematicians. The difficulty in this problem lies in the fact that a ruler and compass only could be used.

If only we could draw a straight line equal to the circumference of circle..... Eureka! But attempts to solve the problem from as far back as 460 B.C. has been in vain.

184 Rakesh was carrying 5 pieces of lumber and Nikhilesh 7. Supposing Nikhilesh had n pieces. If he gave 1 piece to Rakesh, he would have $n - 1$ pieces.

But Rakesh would have then the same number as Nikhilesh. Therefore the total number of pieces must have been:

n – 1 + n – 1 or 2n – 2

Since Nikhilesh had n originally, Rakesh must have had 2n – 2 – n or n – 2.

If Rakesh gave Nikhilesh 1 of his n – 2 pieces, he would have n – 3 and Nikhilesh would have n + 1.

But we have the information that

n + 1 is twice n – 3

i.e.   n + 1 = 2(n – 3)

or   n + 1 = 2n – 6

or   7 = n

        5 = n – 3

185 T, E, T, T, F, F, S, S, E.
First letter of consecutive whole number names.

186 31 Eggs

187

7451	8
3982	4
29 * 69882	8

The numbers at the right of the two factors and the product are the residues after casting out nines.

Since 8 x 4 = 32, the residue on the right of the multiplicant should be 5.

Since 8+7 = 14 residue 5 the missing digit must be 6.

188 About 330

189 Scientists have worked out — though only approximately: Life on earth has existed .....300, 000, 000 years

190 2.3 = 1.2.3   And 14.15 = 5.6.7

191 Knot: A log of thin quadrant of wood was weighed to float upright and fastened to a line wound on a reel, and pieces of knotted string were fastened to the log line.

The number of these knots which ran out while the sand glass was running gave the speed of the ship in knots, or in nautical miles — a nautical mile is 6080 feet — per hour.

192 The diameter of the cherry is three times that of the stone. So, the size of the cherry is $3 \times 3 \times 3 = 27$ times that of the stone.

Thus, the stone occupies 1/27 part of the cherry and the remaining 26/27 part is occupied by the flesh of the cherry.

In other words, the flesh is 26 times bigger in volume than the stone.

193 Let the number of mangoes be X.
The first naughty boy at one, leaving x – 1. He left behind two third of

$$x - 1 \text{ or } \frac{(2x - 1)}{3} \text{ or } \frac{2x - 2}{3}$$

The second naughty boy ate one leaving

$$\frac{2x - 2}{3} - 1$$

$$\text{or } \frac{2x - 2 - 3}{3} \text{ or } \frac{2x - 5}{3}$$

He left behind two-thirds of

$$\text{or } \frac{2x - 5}{3} \text{ or } \frac{2(2x - 5)}{3 \times 3} \text{ or }$$

$$\frac{4x - 10}{9}$$

The third naughty boy ate one, leaving

$$\frac{4x - 19}{9} - 1$$

or $\dfrac{4x - 10 - 9}{9}$ or $\dfrac{4x - 19}{9}$

He left behind two-thirds of

$$\frac{4x - 19}{9} \quad \text{or} \quad \frac{2(4x - 19)}{3 \times 9}$$

or $\dfrac{4x - 38}{27}$

In the morning one mango was eaten leaving

$$\frac{8x - 38}{27} - 1 \quad \text{or} \quad \frac{8x - 38 - 27}{27} \quad \text{or} \quad \frac{8x - 65}{27}$$

Since $\dfrac{8x - 65}{27}$ mangoes were divided equally

into three parts, the number must be a multiple of 3.

Let $\dfrac{8x - 65}{27} = 3n$ where n is an integer.

Then $8x - 65 = 81n$

$8x = 81n + 65$

Since x is a whole number, $81n + 65$ must be an even number, because no odd number is divisible by 8.

Since 65 is odd $81n$ must be odd, because the sum of two odd numbers is even.

Since $81n$ is odd, n must be odd.

Let n be equal to the odd number 2b + 1
Then $8x = 162b + 81 + 65$
or $8x = 162b + 146$
or $4x = 81b + 73$
As before the right side must be even.
Therefore b must be odd.
Let b be equal to the odd number 2c + 1
Then $4x = 162c + 81 + 73$
or $4x = 162c + 154$
or $2x = 81c + 77$
As before the right side must be even.
Therefore c must be odd.
Let c be equal to the odd number 2d + 1
Then $2x = 162d + 81 + 77$
or $2x = 162d + 158$
or $x = 81d + 79$
The least value of x will be obtained when d = 0
Then x = 79
The next value of x can be obtained when x = 1
Then x = 160
The next value of x when d = 3 will be 241.
But by verification 79 will be the correct answer.

194 This is an excellent example of **associativity** for addition:

$S = (1 + - 1) + (1 + - 1) + (1 + - 1)....$
$S = 0 + 0 + 0 + ...$
$S = 0$

However

$S = 1 + (- 1 + 1) + (- 1 + 1) + (- 1 + 1) + ...$
$S = 1 + 0 + 0 + 0 + ...$
$S = 1$

However, if S = 0 and 1 then 2S = 1 and ½
Thus the sum is indeterminate.

195 n $\dfrac{n(n^2 + 1)(n^2 - 1)}{}$

1	0
2	30
3	240
4	1020
5	3120
6	7770
7	16800
8	42760
17	1419840

30 is a factor of each of these numbers. However, when we consider the matter generally:

$n(n^2 + 1)(n^2 - 1) = n^5 - n$

If any digit is raised to the 5th power, the unit's digit in the result is the same as the original digit.

For example $8^5 = 32768$

Therefore, if a number is subtracted from its fifth power, the units digit must be 0.

$6^5 - 6 = 7770$

$9^5 - 9 = 59040$

Generally speaking the units' digit of $n^5 - n$ is zero.

Since $n^2 - 1(n - 1)$, we may write $n(n^2 + 1)(n^2 - 1)$ as $(n - 1)n(n + 1)(n^2 + 1)$

But $n - 1$, n, and $n + 1$ are consecutive numbers.

Therefore their product is an even number. And it has 3 as a factor.

We have already found that $n(n^2 + 1)(n^2 - 1)$ has 5 as a factor.

∴ It must have 6 x 5 or 30 as a factor

196 4. Let the digit unknown be n.
The given number is then $900 + 50 + n = 950 + n$.

When reversed the new number is $100n + 50 + 9 = 59 + 100n$.

Subtracting these two numbers we get $891 - 99n$.

169

The digits can be arranged in 3 ways or 6 ways.
We have already investigated 2 of these ways.
We can now try one of the remaining 4 ways. One of these is n 95

$\therefore 100n + 90 + 5 = 891 - 99n$
or $199n = 796$

$\therefore n = 4$
The unknown digit is 4.

197 The answer is not 30 hours. At the end of 27 hours he is 3 ft from the top. And during the 28th hour he climbs the remaining 3 ft and he is out. So the answer is 28 hours.

198 The farmer's wives made the error of calculating their average price rate by arranging their individual rate of 2 oranges a rupee and 3 oranges a rupee over the same number of apples.

To insure the same takings as those of the first day, they should have determined their price by dividing the total number of oranges by the total number of rupees —that is,

$\dfrac{60}{25}$ or $\dfrac{12}{5}$ oranges a rupee.

They actually sold the oranges at the rate of 2½ oranges a rupee. That's where the missing rupee went.

199 ^{CD}

$$\begin{array}{r} C \ X \ VI \\ X \ III \\ VI \\ CC \ LX \ V \\ \hline CD \end{array}$$

The answer is actually 400. But it is the custom when you use Roman numerals not to write four similar numerals consecutively. Therefore instead of writing four hundreds (C C C C) it is written as one hundred less than five hundred (C D).

Placing the C before the D means C less than D, and placing it after the D, as in DC means C more than D. Hence CD is 400 and DC is 600.

200 (a)
$$\frac{9}{9 \times 9} = 1$$

(b)
$$\frac{9}{9} + 9 = 4$$

(c)
$$\frac{9}{9} + 9 = 6$$

201 The number must be in the form:
N= RK – 1, where R is the least common multiple of 2, 3, 4, 5, 6, 7, 8, and 9.

K = 1, 2, 3 4, ...

R = 2520

N = 2520 – 1;   N = 2519

202 No! The answer is not the express. If we do not take into consideration the length of the train, then slow train and express are the same distance from Calcutta when they meet.

203 About 150,000,000 kilometres.

204 About 17,000,000,000,000 corpuscles

205 About 500 million square kilometres.

206 No, the answer is not Re. 1/-. If the cost of the bottle were Re. 1/- and that of the cork 10P then the bottle would cost only 90P more than the cork. Considering it more carefully we come out with the correct answer : 105 Paise.

207 Turn the magic square around and see. Yes! This is a magic square both upside down and right side up.

208 'Cipher' means Zero. The word 'Cipher' comes from the Arabic **Sifr**. Our word 'Zero' is derived from this word.

209 About 110,000,000 feet.

210 **Three Centimetres:** The book worm only has to go from the front cover of Volume I to the outside of the book cover of Volume III, in other words he only has to travel through Volume II, which is 3 Centimetres.

211 2/15: The two pertinent equations are:
$$B + C = \frac{2}{5}$$
$$\text{and } B = 2C$$

From these we are able to obtain
$$3C = \frac{2}{5} \text{ or } C \frac{2}{15}$$

212 10,000.— Surprised? Well, this is how it works out. It is really immaterial what percentage of the population is one-legged! In any case the one-legged people will all require on shoe per head. From the remaining, half will go barefoot and therefore they need no shoes and the rest will need two shoes per head. And this works out at one shoe per person for the 'others'.

Therefore, we shall need for the whole population on the average one shoe per head.

213 (a) 720. — It may surprise you to see such a big number of arrangements. But it is the product of 6x5x4x3x2x1 that is 6! or 6 — factorial 6.

Here, for example the lefthand lady can be any one of them, so there are 6 ways of choosing her.

The next lady from the lefthand side can be chosen in 5 ways from the remaining 5 ladies.

The next lady in 4 ways from the remaining 4 and the next lady 3 ways and so on.

If there was only one more lady making us 7 ladies together, the number of possible arrangements would be 7 or 5040.

If there were 9 ladies then there would be more than three hundred thousand ways of arranging us.

(b) 120. — Here the situation is entirely different. In this case the answer is not the same as in the case of (a), because it is only the order which is considered here and not the actual position.

In this case there will be 6 positions in which the same order will be found but each position will be turned round relatively to the other.

And there is another way of considering this problem. This is to keep one lady always in the same place and then arrange the remaining 5 ladies. This car be done in 5 ways or 120.

Any order arranged clock-wise has an equivalent order arranged anti-clockwise. So, the number of 120 different ways includes both these as separate arrangements.

214 -3, -1, 1.

215 **Six Dozen Dozen:** Six dozen dozen = 6 x 12 x 12 = 6 x 144 = 864 Half a dozen dozen = 6 x 12 = 72

216

23!	25, 852, 000 000 000 000 000 000
10^{23}	100 000 000 000 000 000 000 000
24!	620, 450, 000 000 000 000 000 000
10^{24}	1,000 000 000 000 000 000 000 000
25!	15,511, 000 000 000 000 000 000 000
10^{25}	10,000 000 000 000 000 000 000 000

Thus the smallest S is 25.

217 Of all the closed plane figures the circle is the biggest. It would be, of course, quite impossible to make a circle out of matches. However, with

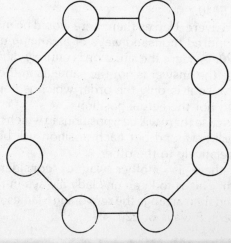

eight matches it is possible to make a figure as shown
in the diagram, which closely resembles a circle — a
regular octagon .

218 $^{12}_{(6)}$ = 924

219 91 or 362880

220 M − x + 1

221 Let us, in order to solve this problem, slit
the cylindrical container open and flatten
out the surface. What we will get is a rectangle whose
width is 20 centimetres and whose length is equal to
the circumference — i e. 10 x 3 1/7 or 31.5
centimetres.

Let us, now, mark in this rectangle the position of
the fly and that of the drop of molasses.

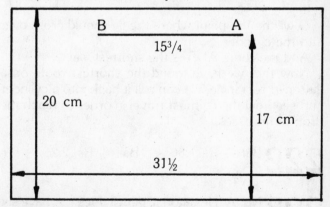

The fly is at point A, that is 17 centimetres from the
base. And the drop of molasses is at point B, which is at

the same height, but half the circumference of the cylinder away from A i.e. 15¾ centimetres away.

To find the point where the fly must climb over the cylinder, we shall have to, from point B draw a perpendicular line to the upper base and continue it upto a similar distance.

This way, we shall obtain C. We shall now connect C by a straight line with point A. Now the diagram should look as below:

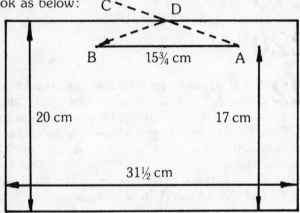

D will be the point where the fly should cross over into the cylinder.

And the route ADB is the shortest way.

Now that we have found the shortest route on a flattened rectangle, we can roll it back into a cylinder and see how the fly must travel in order to reach the drop of molasses.

222 Bat — Rs. 1.50 : Ball — Rs. 2.25

223 No. A 'Hexagonal' pencil does not have six edges as you probably think. It has eight, if not sharpened — six faces and two small bases.

Here the catch is the erroneous interpretation of meaning.

224 The product is 344113. — In the multiplication each cell is the product of the number at the top of each column and to the right of each row, and the sums are added along the diagonals to obtain the final product.

225 Yes. It is possible, we have the correct measurements of its height and base in the photograph.

Let us assume that the height is 95 millimetres and the base 19 millimetres in the photograph. Then we will have to take the measurement of the base of the real tower — which we shall suppose is 15 metres wide.

The tower in the photograph and the real tower are proportionally the same, geometrically. In other words, the ratio between the height and the base of the tower in the photograph is the same as that between the height and the base of the real tower.

In the photograph it is 95 : 19 i.e. 5. So the height of the tower is 5 times greater than the base.

. . The height of the real tower is:
$$15 \times 5 = 75 \text{ Metres}$$

226 $3 \times 3 \times 3 \times 3 \times 3 = 3^5 = 243$. We will have to consider each game separately, because each game may be won, lost or drawn by one of the teams. Therefore there are three possibilities in every game.

The first game has three possibilities and for each one of these possibilities the second game has three possibilities. Therefore there are 9 possible forecasts for the first two games.

For each of the 9 forecasts of the second game, the third game has 3 possibilities, which makes it 27 forecasts and so on.

Therefore for 5 games there are 243 possibilities.

227 7!6! = 10! ; 5!3! = 6! ; 3!5!7! = 10! , 2!47!4! = 48! ; 2!287!4!3! = 288 !

There are many others.

228 **Parallelogram:** A Parallelogram is a rectangle whose angles are no longer right angles, while its opposite sides remain parallel and equal, and its diagonals still bisect the parallelogram into two equal triangle areas. However, its total area will always be less than the area of the rectangle from which it was formed.

229 In a regular chess board there are 1296 rectangles altogether including 8 by 8 outer square.

230 4 rungs only. Boat rises with the tide.

231 We must bear in mind that both pans are geometrically similar bodies. Since the bigger pan is eight times more capacious, all its linear measurements must be two times greater, and it must be twice bigger in height and breadth.

The surface must be 2 x 2 = 4 times greater, because the surface of similar bodies are to one another as the squares of their linear measurements.

Since the wallsides of the pens are of the same thickness, the weight of the pen would depend on the size of its surface. Therefore the answer is —

The bigger pan is four times heavier.

232 1728: The Captain is bound to go crazy deciding the order of rowing in the boat with so many possibilities on hand.

Whichever way you work out the problem you obtain this number 1728.

First of all let us consider the strokeside men first. The fourth oarsman can be chosen from the 3 who can row on either side in 3 ways. And so when this fourth oarsman is chosen the four strokeside oarsman can be arranged in 4! ways. Therefore there are 3 x 4! ways of arranging the strokeside.

Now let us consider the bow side oarsmen. There is no choice of men here, because there are 2 bow side oarsmen and the 2 can row on either side. These two men can be arranged in 4! ways. Because, for each strokeside arrangement any of the bow side arrangements is possible.

Thus the total number of arrangements is

3 x 4! x 4! = 72 x 24 = 1728

233 Approximately 19 years.

234 0 to nine places of decimals 2.71828 1828

235 **1 April:** A female fly lays 120 eggs. Mid–April 120 flies will hatch. **Females: 60**

20 April: 60 female flies lay 120 eggs each Beginning of May 60 x 120 = 7200 flies will hatch.

Females: 3600

5 May: 3600 female flies lay 120 eggs each. Mid–May 3600 x 120 = 43200 flies will hatch.

Females: 216000

25 May: 216000 females flies lay 120 eggs each Beginning of June 216000 x 120 = 25920000 flies will hatch. **Females: 12960000**

14 June: 12960000 female flies lay 120 eggs each End of June 12960000 x 120 = 15552000000 flies will hatch. **Females: 777600000**

15 July: 777600000 female flies lay 120 eggs each Mid–July 777600000 x 120 = 93312000000 flies will hatch. **Females: 46656000000**

25 July: 46656000000 female flies lay 120 eggs each Beginning of August 46656000000 x 120 = 559872000000 will hatch.
Female flies: 27993600000000

13 Aug: 27993600000000 female flies lay 120 eggs each. Last week of August 27993600000000 x 120 = 33592320000000 flies will hatch.

Just in one summer the number of flies that would hatch would be: 33592320000000

Taking each fly to be 5 mm long, if they form a straight line, the distance covered would be 2,500000000 Kilometres — 18 times longer than the distance from the earth to the sun.

236 450 Centimetres. Supposing the tree grows x centimetres each year. Height of the tree at the end of sixth year = (90 + 6x) Cm

Growth in the seventh year $x = \dfrac{1}{9}(90 + 6x)$ Cm

$$x = 10 + \frac{2}{3}x$$

$\therefore \quad x = 30$

The height of the tree at the end of the twelfth year = (90 + 12 x 30) Cm = 450 Cm

P. Paul Lennon
P. Paul Lennon
P. Paul Lennon
P. Paul Lennon
P. Paul Lennon.

1. water collection from Shop = 118m

2. Sweet Purchasing

3. Transphelans

237 127, 255, 511.
This series is being built up according to the order where the actual term = 2n – 1, with n being the number of term.

Eg.,

Ist Term $= 2^1 – 1 = 2 – 1 = 1$
2nd Term $= 2^2 – 1 = 4 – 1 = 3$
3rd Term $= 2^3 – 1 = 8 – 1 = 7$
and so on

238 Let us assume that the average hieght of man is 175 cm. Let us take R as the radius of the earth. Then we have:

$2 \times 3.14 \times (R + 175) – (2 \times 3.14 \times R) = 2 \times 3.14 \times 175 = 1100$ Cm

1100 Cm = 11 Metres

The strange thing you would notice in the problem is the result in no way depends on the radius of the earth.

239 We must, first of all, rotate the small square so that its sides bisect the sides of the large square.

Thus the overlapping area is ¼ of the area of the large square.

$$\left(\frac{1}{4}\right) (17)^2 = \frac{289}{4} = 72\tfrac{1}{4}$$

240 **Carat.** Carat is the standard legal weight for the sale of Diamonds, precious stones and precious metals, since 1878.

A Carat originally weighed 3-1/3 grains but now it weighs 3-1/5 grains. 150 Carats make the Troy ounce of 480 grains.

241 **Checking Addition And Multiplication:** The method of casting out the nines to check the accuracy of additions and multiplications was introduced about a thousand years ago by the Arabs.

To check product of a multiplication nines are 'Cast out' of each factor in the multiplication equation, the remainders are then multiplied and nines are 'Cast out' again. The remainders, if they are unequal at this stage, the multiplication is incorrect.

However, it does not follow that if the remainders are equal the multiplication is correct. But it shows that the chances are that it is correct. So, the process of 'Casting out nines' has only a limited application.

'Casting out nines' can be used to check for mistakes in the addition of numbers also, in the same manner.

242 773, 2753: In this sequence we have to try all the combinations of mathematical operations we know until we find the order which satisfies the sequence. The order in this case is:

$$T_n = 3\,T_{n-1} + 2\,T_{n-2}$$

$$\therefore T_7 = 3 \times 217 + 2 \times 61 = 773$$

243

$$\frac{4+4}{4+4} = 1 \qquad \frac{4+4+4}{\sqrt{4}} = 6$$

$$\frac{4 \times 4}{4+4} = 2 \qquad \frac{44}{4} - 4 = 7$$

$$\frac{4+4+4}{4} = 3 \qquad (4 \times 4) - (4+4) = 8$$

$$\frac{\sqrt{4} + \sqrt{4}}{4} \times 4 = 4 \qquad 4 + 4 + \frac{4}{4} = 9$$

$$\frac{(4 \times 4) + 4}{4} = 5 \qquad \frac{44 - 4}{4} = 10$$

$$\frac{4}{.4} + \frac{4}{4} = 11$$

$$\frac{44 + 4}{4} = 12$$

$$\frac{44}{4} + \sqrt{4} = 13$$

$$4 + 4 + 4 + \sqrt{4} = 14$$

$$\frac{44}{4} + 4 = 15$$

$$4 + 4 + 4 + 4 = 16$$

$$(4 \times 4) + \frac{4}{4} = 17$$

$$4 \times 4 + \frac{4}{\sqrt{4}} = 18$$

$$4! - \left(4 + \frac{4}{4} \right) = 19$$

$$\frac{4 \times 4}{4 \times \sqrt{4}} = 20$$

244 Our holiday lasted for 18 days. First of all let us see how many possible types of days there could be. There could only be three such as:

a) Rain in the morning and fine in the afternoon

b) Fine in the morning and fine in the afternoon

c) Fine in the morning and rain in the afternoon

Let us assume the number of such days in each category be a, b and c.

Then: Number of days on which rain falls = $a + c = 13$

Number of days with fine mornings = $b + c = 11$

Number of days with fine afternoons = $a + b = 12$

We derive from these equations that:

$a = 7$, $b = 5$, $c = 6$

Therefore the number of days on holiday is:

$$7 + 5 + 6 + 18$$

245 Neither. There is same amount in each. Let us assume:

a = amount of orangeade in glass at start

b = amount of orangeade first transferred.

c = amount of orangeade transferred second time

d = amount of Lemonade transferred to orangeade

Now we must show that the amount of Lemonade in orangeade equals the amount of orangeade in the Lemonade or, in terms of a, b, c, d we must show that:

$$d = b - c$$

Time	Amount of Orangeade in Glass
Start	a
1st Transfer	a – b
2nd Transfer	(a – b) + (c + d)

184

The starting amount, a, must equal the final amount after the second transfer.

$\therefore$ a = (a – b) + c + d or d = b – c

246 $\dfrac{1}{2^{24}} = \dfrac{1}{16777216}$

247 1 googolplex = 10 googol = 1 followed by a googol of zeroes = 100 000 000 000 000 000 000 000 000 000 000 000 000 000 000 000 000 000 000 000 000 000 000 000 000 000 000 000 000 00

248 5–5/11 minutes past 7.

Exactly at 7 O'clock the minute hand is 35 divisions behind the hour hand. In order to be opposite one another the minute hand must gain 5 divisions on the hour hand.

However, the minute hand gains 35 divisions in 60 true minutes.

And therefore the minute hand gains 5 divisions in 5–5/11 true minutes.

249 **Secant:** When a straight line cuts any curve at two distinct points, it is called a Secant. However, Secant is not the same as tangent. Tangent, no matter how far it is produced either way, has only one point in common with the curve.

250 Cardioid is a curve shaped like a heart.

251 Ramu is 18 years old.

24 – x years ago Lakshmi was x years old and now she is 24.

24 – x years ago Ramu was x – (24 – x) years old.

Today he is x years old.

24 = 2 (2x – 24)

∴ x = 8

252 Cube:
A hexahedron is a solid figure which has six faces. And a regular hexahedron is a cube, because it has six equal faces.

253 Inscribed:
In a polygon when each side is tangential to a circle, the circle is said to be inscribed in a polygon.

The inscribed circle is obtained by bisecting the angles of the triangle, where the bisectors pass through a common point which is the centre of the inscribed circle.

254

Sin 45°	$\dfrac{1}{\sqrt{2}}$	Cot 45°	1
Cos 45°	$\dfrac{1}{\sqrt{2}}$	Sec 45°	$\sqrt{2}$
Tan 45°	1	Csc 45°	$\sqrt{2}$

255

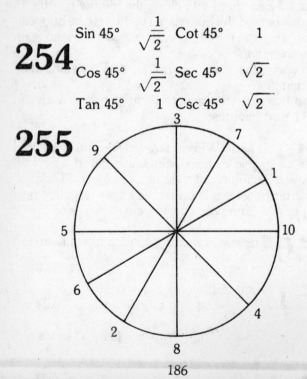

256 **Seven:** The best way to find the solution to this problem is to make a practical experiment.

Make a vertical cut in the tree trunk and peel off the trunk to form a long rectangle. Across the rectangle draw 5 parallel lines to represent the jasmine and another parallel line for the rose. Then you will be able to see the seven crossing positions.

257 **36:** The first die may fall in six different ways. With each of these ways there are 6 possibilities for the second die.

258 P = 2q – 5

259 40

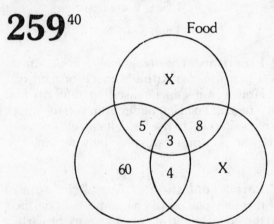

Let us assume the number who complained about food only be x.

Those with complaints= 160

$$\therefore 2x + 80 \qquad = 160$$
$$\therefore \qquad x \qquad = 40$$

260 From the top clockwise: 10, 1, 11, 7, 4, 6, 12, 2, 8, 5, 9, 3.

261 **Centroid:** The three times from a vertex to the mid–point of the opposite side (Medians) of a triangle pass through a common point called the Centroid of the triangle. The term is derived from 'Centre' and 'Oid' the centre of gravity of a triangular lamina is at this point.

262 **Approximating an area:** Simpson's rule is put to use when the area is divided into any even number of parallel strips of equal breadth.

263 **2420 Feet:** $\dfrac{1100 \text{ ft.}}{1 \text{ Sec}} = \dfrac{x \text{ ft.}}{(11/5) \text{ Sec}}$

Then x = 2420

264 **Frustrum:** The technical translation of 'Frustrum' would be 'a piece broken off'.
However it can be used to refer to that portion of a regular solid left after cutting off the upper part by a plane parallel to the base. It can also be used to describe the portion intercepted between any two planes.

265 **Parallel of Latitude:** A small circle drawn through places of the same latitude, it is parallel to the equator and at right angles to the earth's axis or the line joining the North and South Poles.

266 The farmer was pointing at the basket with 29 eggs. Chicken eggs were in the basket marked 23, 12 and 5. Duck eggs were in the basket marked 14 and 6.
To verify the answer

23 + 12 + 5 + 40 chicken eggs after the transaction and 14 + 6 = duck eggs.

There were twice as many chicken eggs as duck eggs, as the problem said.

267 K = 1

268 Hexagon: The open end of the bees cell has a hexagonal shape. This is a familiar sight to all of us.

The hexagon of the bee's cell is one of the few regular shapes that can completely fill the space on a bee frame. One can't but help reaching the conclusion that bees have a certain geometrical aptitude or sense.

269 9.40 and 41 Metres: To check the solution: Square the length of the perpendicular, subtract 1 and divide by 2, and the result is the length of the base. Add 1 to this and this same formula applies when the perpendicular is any odd number and these combinations of numbers are sometimes called 'Pythogorean' series.

This method is derived from the theorem of Pythagoras concerning the right angled triangle.

$$H^2 = B^2 + p^2$$
$$\therefore (B + 1)^2 = B^2 + P^2$$
$$\therefore 28 + 1 = P^2$$

$$\therefore B = \frac{P^2 - 1}{2}$$

In this case B = $\frac{9^2 - 1}{2}$ = 40 Metres

We are told that H = B + 1
$$\therefore H = 41 \text{ Metres.}$$

270 **Pedal:** This triangle is also called the Orthocentric triangle.

If AD, BE and CF are the perpendiculars dropped from the vertices of the triangle ABC to the opposite sides, then the triangle DEF is the pedal triangle.

The three perpendiculars pass through a common point called the Orthocentre.

271 The first piece can be placed in any of the 64 squares. In other words, there are 64 ways of placing it. Now remains 63 squares for the second piece, that is to any one of the 64 positions of the first piece we can add the 63 positions to the second.

∴ There are 64 x 63 = 4032 different positions in which two pieces may be placed on a draught board.

272 **Pascal's:** Pascal built up the rows of Numeral 11, 121, 1331, 14641, etc. that can be enclosed by a triangle. These numerals not only give the coefficients for certain binomial expansions, and can also be used to solve problems in Statistics dealing with probability.

273 12 x 5 = 60 faces.

274 At the rate of Re. 1/- for ten weeks we figure that the amount of interest for one year would be Rs. 5.20. But I do not have the use of my Rs. 10/- for the entire period of time — but on the average just half that amount. So we conclude that I paid Rs. 5.20 to use Rs. 5/- for one year.

$$\frac{5.2}{5} = \frac{104}{100} = 104\%$$

∴ The true simple annual interest is 104%.

275 This job can be done simply by opening up only three links — the links of one section, and joining the ends of the other four sections with them.

276 **Arc of a Cycloid:** The Bernoullis are responsible for the name of the problem. And it refers to the well known brachistochrome problem or the curve on which a body descending to a given point under the action of gravity will reach it in the shortest time.

277 The 9th triangular number = Sum of first 9 natural numbers.

The 10th triangular number = Sum of first 10 natural numbers.

The nth triangular number = Sum of first n natural numbers = $\dfrac{n(n+1)}{2}$

278 3, 10, 17, 24, 31, 38, 45, 52, 54 and 66. The series formed is an arithmetical progression with a common difference of 7.

279 A square metre equals 1000 square millimetres. One thousand millimetre squares placed one alongside the other will stretch out 1 metre.

∴ 1000 squares will be 1000 metres long
In other words 1000 kilometres long.

280 **44 Centimetres:** Many a time steel bars are used as rollers in this way.
The safe moves forward twice the length of the circumference of one of the steel bars.

∴ This distance is $\dfrac{2.22.7}{7}$ Cm.

And this is 44 Centimetres.

Three or for that matter any number of rollers under the safe will move the safe 44 centimetres forward.

In order to see the problem more clearly, let us consider this problem in two parts:

(a) The motion forward caused by one revolution of the rollers if they were rolling off the ground.

(b) The motion forward of the centres of the rollers because they themselves roll forward on the ground.

The motion amounts to 22 centimetres in both cases. So, the total movement of the safe mounted on the rolling rollers is 44 centimetres.

281

630 Litres: Let us assume x is the capacity of the second barrel.

Then our equation will be:

$$\frac{5}{6} \times 336 = \frac{4}{9} \times X$$

$$\therefore X = \frac{5 \times 336 \times 9}{6 \times 1 \times 4} = 630$$

282

Tripods are so convenient for land surveying instruments and photographic cameras, because the tripod stands firmly on three legs. The three legs of a tripod always rest on the floor because through any three points of space there can pass one

192

plane. And only one. The reason is purely geometrical and not physical.

283 56 women and 40 men: To solve this problem we need to put the story–down in mathematical symbols.

W– 16 =　M
7W – 32 = 9M
Multiplying line 1 by 9, we obtain:
9W – 144 = 9M
Taking away line 2 from line 3 we get:
2W – 112 = 0
W　　　= 56
M　　= 40

284 **Square:** the 'Great Square of Pegasus' stands out distinctly in a very obvious shape in the heavens, because all four stand at the corners are bright and there are no bright stars within the square.

During the period of the September equinox, it is clearly seen in the northern hemisphere almost due south at midnight.

285 18. — Rajiv scores 50 whilst Sanjiv scores 40, Sanjiv scores 50 whilst Vijay scores 40 Sanjiv scores 40 whilst Vijay scores

$$\frac{40 \times 40}{50} = 32$$

∴ Rajiv scores 50 whilst Sanjiv scores 40 and whilst Vijay scores 32.

∴ Rajiv can give 18 points to Vijay.

286 There are altogether 70 ways of going from A to B.

287 **About Nine Centimetres:** The needle moves from the outermost groove to the innermost groove in an arc. The radius of this arc is the length of the pick–up arm.

288 Greatest: Log 2 + Log 4: Smallest: Log 6 + Log 3

Log (2 + 4) = Log 6
Log 2 + Log 4 = Log (2 x 4) = Log 8
Log (6 – 3) = Log 3
Log 6 – Log 3 = Log 6 ÷ 3 = Log 2

Log 8 is the greatest and Log 2 is the least of these values.

289 4900

290 Length of the train 80 metres, Length of the tunnel 800 metres.

Length of the train = 96 x $\dfrac{3}{60 \times 60}$ Km = 80 metres

Length of the tunnel = $\dfrac{96 \times 30}{60 \times 60}$ Km = 800 metres.

291 Four. Most people think the answer is three, because it is easy to create an equilateral triangle with a tree planted on each corner. But if the land had just the right contours, a fourth tree might be planted in a valley or on a hill, forming a pyramid shape above or below the centre of the triangle in a spot that would maintain the equidistance.

292 **Prime Numbers:** Erastosthenes, a contemporary of Archimedes, constructed an instrument to duplicate a cube and gave a laborious method of constructing a table of prime numbers. This is called the 'Sieve of Erastosthenes.'

293

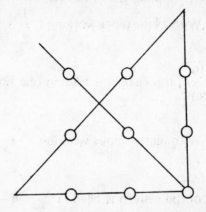

294 II.—The value of the given series is approximately 0.76. And when two more terms are added the value approximates to 0.77. When we multiply these values by 4, we get 3.04 and 3.08. If this is repeated indefinitely we shall approach the value of 3.14.

3.14 is the value of II correct to two places of decimals.

295 26 x 25 x 4 = 15600. — This is an example of 'Permutation of 26 different letters taken 3 at a time'. It is written in mathematical language as 26 p3

It is easy to arrive at this calculation really, when expressed in terms of factorials. It is the result of dividing factorial 26 by factorial (26 –3).

Generally speaking the number of permutations of n things if only r are taken at any one time is or factorial n divided by factorial (n –r) $^n p^r$

195

296 $1\dfrac{11}{19}$ Hours. In one hour S fills 1/2 K fills 1/3 and Y empties 1/5 of the cistern.

∴With all the pipes working ($\dfrac{1}{2} + \dfrac{1}{3} - \dfrac{1}{5}$)

Or $\dfrac{19}{30}$ of the cistern is filled in one hour.

∴With all the pipes working $\left(\dfrac{30}{30}\right)$

of the cistern is filled in $\left(\dfrac{30}{19}\right)$ hours.

297 1024/11 times.

			R has left	S has left
		End of one drink	½	½
$\dfrac{1}{11}$	$\dfrac{1}{2^{10}}$	End of two drinks	$\dfrac{1}{3}$	$(½)^2$
		End of three drinks	¼	$(½)^3$
		End of four drinks	$\dfrac{1}{5}$	$(½)^4$
		End of five drinks	$\dfrac{1}{6}$	$(½)^5$

| End of six drinks | $\dfrac{1}{7}$ | $(\frac{1}{2})^6$ |

$$\dfrac{2^{10}}{11} = \dfrac{1024}{11}$$

End of seven drinks	$\dfrac{1}{8}$	$(\frac{1}{2})^7$
End of eight drinks	$\dfrac{1}{9}$	$(\frac{1}{2})^8$
End of nine drinks	$\dfrac{1}{10}$	$(\frac{1}{2})^9$
End of ten drinks	$\dfrac{1}{11}$	$(\frac{1}{2})^{10}$

298 **180 Metres:** The linear measurements of the object are to the corresponding measurements of the picture as the distance of the object from the lens is to the depth of the camera.

Let X be the height of the plane, in metres. Then we come to the following proportion:

12000: 8 = X: 0, 12

∴ X = 180 metres

299 **71.4 Metres:** Sanjiv runs 1470 metres while Vijay runs 1400 metres.

At the same rate Sanjiv runs 1500 metres whilst Vijay runs

$$\dfrac{1500 \times 1400}{1470} \text{ Metres}$$

or   1428.6 metres

Hence Sanjiv ought to beat Vijay by 71.4 metres.

300 120: This problem is an example of the multiplicative principle. Here there are 12 ways of choosing the Secretary. With each of these ways it is possible to choose the Joint Secretary in 10 ways. The particular woman who is chosen as the Joint Secretary is not determined by the choice of the Secretary. The choice of each is made independently and in succession. Therefore the total number of possibilities is the product of the two possibilities.

301 My plane did not fly along the contours of a square because the earth is round and the meridians converge at the pole.

Therefore when I flew 500 km along the parallel, 500 kilometres north of Leningrad latitude, my plane covered more degrees going eastward than it did when it was returning along Leningrad latitude. As a result, my aircraft completed its flight east of Leningrad.

Now the question is, how many kilometres?

That can be easily calculated.

The diagram also shows the route taken by my aircraft ABCD.

N is the North Pole where meridians AB and DC meet.

My plane first flew 500 km northward i.e. along meridian AN. Since the degree of a meridian is 111 kilometres long, the 500 kilometre long arc of the meridian is equal to $500 : 111 = 4°5'$.

Leningrad lies on the 60th parallel. Therefore B is on $60° + 4°5' = 64°5'$.

The aircraft then flew eastward i.e. along the BC parallel, covering 500 kilometres.

The length of one degree of this parallel is equal to 48 kilometres.

Therefore, we can easily determine how many degrees my aircraft covered in its eastward flight : $500 : 48 + 10°4'$.

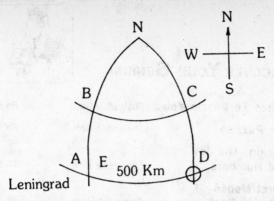

Continuing my aircraft flew southward i.e. along meridian CD, and having covered 500 km returned to the Leningrad parallel. Then the way lay westward i.e. along D.A.

Obviously, the 500 kilometres along DA are less than the distance between A and D.

However there are as many degrees in AD as in BC, i.e. 10°4'. But the length of 1° at the 60th parallel equals 55.5 kilometres.

Hence the distance between A and D is equal to 55.5 x 10.4 = 577 kilometres.

So my plane could not have very well landed in Leningrad. It landed 77 kilometres away, on Lake Lagoda.